A Brief History of
Critical Infrastructure Protection
in the United States

# Critical Path

KATHI ANN BROWN

Foreword by John A. McCarthy,
Critical Infrastructure Protection Program, George Mason University

First printing, June 2006

Designed and published by
Spectrum Publishing Group, Inc.
Fairfax, Virginia
www.spgidesign.com

Printed in the United States of America

This research was supported by grant #60NANB2D0108 from the
National Institute of Standards and Technology (NIST) through the
Critical Infrastructure Protection (CIP) Program at George Mason
University. Any opinions, findings, and recommendations expressed in
this material are those of the authors and do not necessarily reflect the
views of NIST or CIP Program.

Dedicated to the Commissioners and staff of the President's
Commission on Critical Infrastructure Protection and to the many
patriotic owners and operators of the nation's critical infrastructure
who have worked to actualize the Commission's findings and
make the country safer.

"The measures and countermeasures game is never over. As you develop a capability, obviously it will have weaknesses. Then, as the enemy—or whatever—exploits those weaknesses, why, you figure out ways to counter those exploitations. It's never-ending."

General Robert T. Marsh
President's Commission on Critical Infrastructure Protection
Oral history interview, March 17, 2004

# Table of Contents

# Preface

I n the fall of 2003, the Center for History and New Media (CHNM) at George Mason University was invited by the Critical Infrastructure Protection Program (CIPP), also affiliated with GMU, to undertake a special oral history program to document the evolution of the nation's critical infrastructure protection policy. We were delighted to accept. Two years earlier, the events of September 11, 2001 had set in motion a major reorganization of the federal government's emergency response system and had ignited a national conversation about security and defense issues. The timing seemed right to begin capturing and archiving some of the early thinking about critical infrastructure protection that preceded creation of the Department of Homeland Security in November 2002. These issues were of particular interest to CHNM because of our work in creating the September 11 Digital Archive, which became the premiere online repository of information related to the 9/11/2001 attacks.

A natural focal point for the first phase of the oral history project was the President's Commission on Critical Infrastructure Protection (PCCIP), created in the summer of 1996 by President Bill Clinton, partly in response to the bombing of the Murrah Federal Building in Oklahoma City the previous year. Deliberate destruction of a little-known federal building, located far outside the "nerve center" of Washington, D.C., set off a chain reaction of events and effects that reverberated well beyond Oklahoma City. Government officials quickly realized that the toll on human life and the building itself was compounded by the crippling of key functions. From the loss of a payroll department to the devastation of a wing of the FBI, damage from the bomb was felt from coast-to-coast by other government agencies, employees and/or the private sector in ways previously unimagined.

On the recommendation of an interagency group chaired by Attorney

General Janet Reno, Clinton gave the PCCIP a mandate to study the complexities of the nation's critical infrastructures and issue recommendations for improving their security. Chaired by General Robert T. Marsh, the PCCIP included a number of senior-level government officials, private industry executives, and leaders from the academic community. The group deliberated for fifteen months and in October 1997 issued its final report: *Critical Foundations: Protecting America's Infrastructures.*

As John McCarthy notes in his Introduction to *Critical Path*, the PCCIP's work marked an important, if quiet, shift in thinking about national security and defense. CHNM was especially fortunate to interview many of the key figures on the PCCIP, as well as others who helped to implement the Commission's recommendations. By capturing their insights for the record we hope to make their experience and expertise of use and value to all who follow in their footsteps.

Roy Rosenzweig
Director, Center for History and New Media
George Mason University
January 2006

# Foreword

Critical paths are seldom known in advance—where they lead, who is charting them, and will anyone follow? The history of infrastructure protection, as recounted in this book, examines a number of these paths and in particular, the findings of a small, little noticed group, the *President's Commission on Critical Infrastructure Protection* (PCCIP), chartered to examine the broader security, technical and policy implications of the Oklahoma City bombing. Their findings, entitled *"Critical Foundations: Protecting America's Infrastructures"*, published in 1997, helped create a new understanding of our strengths and weaknesses as a nation. The principles they outlined became entering arguments in the debate over our post 9/11 vulnerabilities and have helped redefine our national and economic security in the information age.

Since the American Revolution, our greatest leaders have recognized that a key indicator of national strength is the development and maintenance of an advanced system of infrastructures. Our extensive built infrastructures—postal, banking, roads, water, and pipelines, among others—moved us from an agricultural society to a manufacturing powerhouse and marked us as the most advanced nation on earth in the industrial age. The recent emergence of complex and sophisticated information infrastructures comprised of global computer networks and highly advanced control systems, have propelled us into the twenty-first century and have enabled pre-existing infrastructures to operate at enhanced levels with astounding results. Additionally, these enormous technological gains have had an immense impact on our culture in general. Like the threats to the infrastructures themselves, these simple facts have had an enormous cascading impact on the way we operate as a society and on our understanding of law, policy, economics, and business. However, in the process of advancing our national capacity and economic strength, a greater dependence on these technologies has created hidden interdependencies making us more vulnerable during both natural and man-made disaster.

In his landmark work, *"The Structure of Scientific Revolutions"*, Thomas Kuhn argued that the progress of science is not incremental but revolutionary in the sense of a "punctuated equilibrium". This is where change occurs rapidly, but comes amidst long periods of fixed thought. Kuhn called these revolutionary processes "paradigm shifts", a term that is now used to describe a profound change in our frame of reference, be it science, commerce, or policy. This change is by no means linear. Kuhn argues that the assimilation of such new worldviews into the mainstream "requires the reconstruction of prior theory and the re-evaluation of prior fact, an intrinsically revolutionary process that is seldom completed by a single man and never overnight."[1]

The findings of the PCCIP can be interpreted in a similar way—as the catalyst for radical rethinking of fundamental constructs of security and economics frozen in 40 years of Cold War assumptions. In less than a decade following the publication of *"Critical Foundations"*, it can be argued that we have seen Kuhn's change process dramatically unfold— conceptualized by PCCIP in the late 1990s, galvanized in the changes implemented by government and industry leaders in the wake of September 11, 2001, and personalized by the public at large in the destructive aftermath of Hurricanes Katrina and Rita in 2005.

In May of 2001, prior to the tragedy of September 11, leaders at George Mason University School of Law began a dialogue with Congressman Frank Wolf of Virginia, a forward thinking House member on security and infrastructure issues. The purpose of this discussion was to create a research program that examined the legal, policy, economic and technical implications of critical infrastructure protection (CIP) on our nation. Through Congressman Wolf's sponsorship and guidance, the National Institute of Standards and Technology was designated the exec- utive agent and the Mason CIP Program was born. I joined the Program as the first Director in April 2002, with the charge to build one of the nation's first interdisciplinary, multi-institutional programs that treated critical infrastructure as a discipline. One of the initial research goals I out- lined for the CIP Program was to capture and analyze important themes and lessons learned from infrastructure development over time, particu- larly during the seminal decade—1990. Partnering with the George Mason University Center for History and New Media, we sought to undertake an effort using an oral history methodology to capture the experience of those engaged in this effort.

We invited the PCCIP Chair, General Robert T. Marsh, USAF (*ret*), former Commissioners, selected staff and several players key to the Commissions formation to sit down with us and share their thoughts about "*Critical Foundations*" and its implications. The nineteen people who accepted our invitation gave us a total of approximately fifty hours of recorded interviews, which generated nearly 1,000 pages of transcripts. The second half of this book draws heavily on the interviews to explore and highlight the Commission's work, including the sometimes challenging—but never dull—process its members used to come to their conclusions.

Our intention in putting together this short volume went beyond documenting the work of the PCCIP alone, however. Organizations rarely operate in a vacuum, and the PCCIP was no exception. The national debate about how best to protect the country, its people and its assets has been ongoing for more than two centuries. One of the biggest issues has been the proper role of the federal government. From patrolling post roads in the eighteenth century, to waging the Cold War, to blocking Internet hackers, federal responsibility to provide for "the common defense" has shifted and evolved according to each era's perceived threats.

The brief history presented here does not pretend to be a definitive look at the robust and frequently contentious debate that accompanies major policymaking in the federal government. Able scholars have dissected virtually every aspect of every era of past decision-making about national security and homeland defense. Instead, we have tried to supply a lively, succinct historical context for understanding some of the national security issues and challenges that face us today. In doing so, we hope to provide policymakers and other players in the critical infrastructure arena with a handy and valuable tool for thinking about current and future policymaking.

Ultimately, full transcripts of all of the interviews developed by the program will be available at the Special Collections & Archives division of George Mason University's Fenwick Library, as well as on the CIP Program's website http://cipp.gmu.edu. We are also putting together an online archive of selected primary source documents that will illuminate recent thinking about the intersection between critical infrastructure and national security.

The CIP Program is particularly indebted to the talented research and authorship of Ms. Kathi Ann Brown of Milestones Historical Consultants, who took the concept and goals of this project and made them a reality in this book. Kathi was assisted by Ms. Rebecca Luria Phillips, a Research Assistant for the Center for History and New Media, who provided in-depth historical research and had the laborious task of conducting the interviews and editing the many interview transcripts that contributed to the oral history this publication captures. Of additional note were Drs. Roy Rosenzweig and Tom Scheinfeldt, who manage Mason's Center for History and New Media (CHNM), for their overall support and guidance.

In particular, I would also like to recognize General Tom Marsh, Mr. Phil Lacombe, and Ms. Nancy Wong who helped us organize this entire effort and gain access to individuals, documents and pictures that assisted in the research. Also, thanks are extended to my friend, Mr. Lee Zeichner, who worked tirelessly behind the scenes providing considerable guidance and energy.

"*Critical Foundations*" articulated a redefinition of the relationship between government, private sector and academe in support of a revolutionary national security agenda. The Mason CIP Program has sought to actualize this important national priority. This book is dedicated to the groundbreaking work of the Commissioners and staff of the President's Commission on Critical Infrastructure Protection who helped chart and guide all of us down a new path towards enhanced homeland security.

John A. McCarthy, Director
Critical Infrastructure Protection Program
George Mason University School of Law
January 2006

---

[i] Kuhn, Thomas S. (1962). The Structure of Scientific Revolutions. 3rd Ed, 1996. Chicago: University of Chicago Press, p.7.

# Introduction

*"Certain national infrastructures are so vital that
their incapacity or destruction would have
a debilitating impact on the defense or
economic security of the United States."*

Executive Order 13010
President William J. Clinton
July 15, 1996

A quick Google search in 2005 using the term critical infrastructure turns up 650,000 hits, including a wealth of articles and documents. Dig a little deeper into proprietary databases, library catalogs, think tank reports and books, and even more material surfaces.

What's the fuss about? What is critical infrastructure? Pose the question to the average American and the response is likely to be a blank stare or bemused shrug. But mention water supplies, the electrical grid, banking networks, air traffic control or oil pipelines—and understanding dawns.

The term critical infrastructure—or CI—is relatively new, and its definition elusive and evolving. On the other hand, threats to services and systems that are important to human activity have always been with us, long before *critical infrastructure* became a term of art in policymaking circles.

One of the most obvious—and longest-running—threats to critical infrastructure is Mother Nature, who delivers her message in the form of fires, floods, hurricanes, fallen trees, curious squirrels, earthquakes, lightning and other forces. Anyone whose flight out has been cancelled due to bad weather, or who has driven miles out of the way to avoid a washed-out bridge, knows that nature has its ways of reminding us of who's boss.

Simple wear-and-tear also poses a constant challenge to critical infrastructure. In the 1980s, a great deal of federal-level attention was devoted to discussing the deteriorating state of the nation's physical infrastructure—the roads, bridges, dams, airports, and similar systems upon which the country depends. The problem is not a small one: nearly four million miles of roadway alone crisscross the country. In its 1988 final report, *Fragile Foundations: A Report on America's Public Works*, a national council gave the nation's infrastructure a C-, "hardly something the world's largest industrial power can be proud of."[i] Upkeep, much less expansion, presents an enormous and ongoing infrastructure chore.

Other problems that can plague critical infrastructure include technological obsolescence, poor maintenance, accidents, or that perennial peril: human error. "There are more communications systems taken down per day by the backhoe than by anybody else," notes one infrastructure expert with a touch of humor.

Last, but far from least, intentional destruction of critical infrastructure has always been an issue, albeit a fairly low-key concern during peacetime, until September 11, 2001, when it jumped to the top of the list of federal priorities. It is this last category of potential disruption that has prompted the most recent flurry of federal-level discussion and policymaking related to the nation's infrastructure (and hence, this book).

The strategy of targeting an adversary's vital systems or services for destruction by sabotage or outright attack is far from novel. History offers abundant examples of stratagems designed either to protect one's own critical infrastructure from peril or to destroy that belonging to an adversary, especially during times of war.

To offer but two examples, in ancient Greece, one of Sparta's head warriors, Lysander, seized the Hellespont, the main source of grain imports for Athens, a strategy calculated to starve the city into submission. A weakened Athens tried to fight back but was decisively defeated at Aegospotami. In 1943, the "Casablanca directive" laid out an Allied strategic bombing campaign designed to bring about "the progressive destruction of the German military and industrial and economic system, and the undermining of the morale of the German people to a point where their capacity for armed resistance is fatally weakened."[ii] Allied bombing attacks on Germany's railway system after D-Day in 1944 destroyed approximately two-thirds of German rolling stock, slowing delivery of finished goods to the point that the nation's economy was pushed towards collapse.

The main goal, of course, is to destroy—or at least cripple—an adversary's ability to fight, to resupply itself, to communicate, and to function normally. The anthrax scare that shut down a U.S. Senate Office Building in late 2001, for example, appears to have been an attempt to hobble critical infrastructure—in this case, the operations of government.

Destruction isn't always limited to the "enemy's" critical infrastructure. The history of warfare offers many examples of intentional destruction of components of one's own infrastructure—blowing up bridges, for example, to short-circuit the advance of the enemy. Of course, military history also touts the exploits of outfits specially trained to repair or replace such destroyed structures on demand. The U.S. Army's Corps of Engineers excels at throwing bridges across rivers virtually overnight. Their successes at building infrastructure on demand in World War II led General Douglas MacArthur to dub the conflict "an engineer's war."

Naturally, there's a flipside to all of these potential dangers and destructive forces: It's the *defense* of critical infrastructure, or what is today called *critical infrastructure protection* or CIP.

Critical infrastructure protection includes wide-ranging efforts to fortify, insulate and, if need be, quickly repair, rebuild or replace vital systems and services. A few conventional examples include security checkpoints, system redundancies, regularly scheduled back-ups, and preventive maintenance. Even the "Miss Utility" program of areas like Washington, D.C. is an exercise in CIP: the program is designed to keep homeowners from hitting gas, electrical and water lines when excavating for the family swimming pool.

Beginning in the 1980s, the growing use of computers in business and government—combined with the easy accessibility of the burgeoning Internet—added a fresh dimension (and increased urgency) to CIP. Quietly but quickly, much of the nation's most basic infrastructure (e.g. utilities, transportation, banking) came to depend on computers to control many basic functions. Suddenly, not only was the physical infrastructure itself vulnerable to conventional methods of destruction such as explosives, but the overlay of high-tech networks that controlled them was also a potential target of would-be terrorists, criminals, disaffected employees . . . and bored teenagers equipped with a laptop and ample leisure-time.

Says Phil Lacombe, who worked with the President's Commission on Critical Infrastructure Protection: "We didn't realize that as you pursue the tremendous economic benefits of information systems, you are creating vulnerabilities and dependencies that carried their own seeds of destruction.

. . . It was a revelation for some of the commissioners, as well as for others, that our water systems rely on computer networks and telephone—the ability to use a telephone to dial in to perform maintenance on the water supply system. I didn't think about that stuff before."

Lacombe was far from alone. Most people—except those on the "front lines"—would have had little reason to think about, much less worry about, the perils of increasing interconnectedness. Or to be concerned about how such interconnectedness might prove to be an *Achilles heel in the nation's otherwise formidable defenses.*

"[B]ecause of our cyber dependence, [groups] now had a way of attacking the nation without ever encountering the nation's defense forces," notes Lacombe. "You couldn't fly a bomber at the United States without encountering a radar warning system. You couldn't fire a missile at the United States, anywhere in the world, without encountering a space-based detection capability. You could, however, launch what we called a logic bomb. There are all kinds of names for them, but you could launch an attack, a cyber attack, without ever encountering anything except the public switch network, the Internet, and the World Wide Web."

"We no longer mobilize for war the way we used to," points out Lee Zeichner, a security consultant. "Everything depends on critical infrastructure—soldiers fly out on United Airlines and we use Federal Express. It's so intertwined in how we live that it's a national defense issue."

## ENTER PUBLIC POLICY-MAKING.

Because the principal goal of this book is to shed light on the evolution of *federal-level* CIP policy-making, it's useful to place the critical infrastructure protection story within the larger story of how the federal government has responded (or not responded) to (perceived or real) threats to critical infrastructure over the past two centuries and more.

Doing so requires looking at the overall picture of the nation's attitude and actions to protect itself, especially on its home turf, in response to changes in adversaries, weaponry, citizen demands and domestic politics. A common umbrella term for this effort is *preparedness*.

Not surprisingly, the most visible and vociferous public debates about the nation's level of preparedness have come during times of major disasters or heightened fears of attack. Examples include: during World Wars I and II, after the U.S.S.R. successfully detonated an atomic bomb in 1949 and a hydrogen bomb in 1953, following the Cuban Missile Crisis of 1962, and after the events of September 11, 2001.

Among the "big" questions that have driven the national preparedness debate since the beginning are such sticky issues as how much preparedness is enough? How much is too much? What's worth protecting? At what cost? Whose responsibility is it, anyway? Federal? State? Local? Private? And who's going to ante up?

Today, post-September 11, the debate over the appropriate level of general preparedness (now called homeland defense or homeland security) is once again raising controversial questions about the quality and quantity of laws, regulations and resources that should be devoted to 'securing security.' As well as the costs and responsibilities/roles of various parties. Naturally, the nation's critical infrastructure and its protection are part of this larger debate.

This slim volume doesn't pretend to paint a full-blown and detailed picture of American preparedness policy since the nation's founding. Scholars have devoted thousands of pages to examining such policy-making in minute detail. Instead, we offer a primer, one that will paint the proverbial "big picture" of preparedness policy, while encouraging inquisitive readers to delve into specifics via the bibliography and materials that can be found on our CIP Oral History website: URL: http://echo.gmu.edu/cipp.

In these pages, we highlight key events and developments in the evolution of official thinking on such (often overlapping) preparedness issues as civil defense, industrial mobilization, and emergency management—up to and including the work of the President's Commission on Critical Infrastructure Protection (1996–1997), where our story ends.

In the process, we'll touch on factors that have informed the CIP debate over time. For example:

- Changes in what is considered critical infrastructure. How our perception of "critical" has changed or remained the same over the past three centuries.
- The (often inherently) conflicting agendas of public and private sector interests in the level and types of security devoted to critical infrastructure.
- The fact that the majority of the nation's CI is in private—not governmental—hands, which raises the sticky question of proper roles and responsibilities of federal, state, local government and the private sector in CIP.
- Modes of making and delivering threats. How evolving technologies have altered the ways in which nation states, groups or individuals can threaten populations, undermine public confidence, disrupt or compromise critical systems.

And, finally, the human response to threats: How fear and complacency have influenced public willingness over time to support or question governmental initiatives to institute policies in the name of "national security."

---

[i] National Council on Public Works Improvement, Fragile foundations: a report on America's public works: final report to the President and the Congress (Washington: GPO, 1988): 2.

[ii] Gerhard L. Weinberg, A World at Arms. A Global History of World War II (Cambridge: Cambridge University Press, 1994).

# CHAPTER 1

# From the Post Roads of the 1790s to the Great War of 1914:

## The First Century of Critical Infrastructure in the United States

*99,000 miles of railroad track*

*19,500 airports*

*160,000 miles of oil pipelines*

*More than 1,000,000 miles of gas pipelines*

*More than 4,000,000 miles of roads*

*590,000 bridges*

*79,000 dams*

*182,000,000 wireless subscriptions*

*380,000 ATMs*

I n the first decade of the twenty-first century, it requires a fertile imagination to block out the high-tech signs of modern life and conjure up an image of the decidedly low-tech United States of three centuries ago.

*…Buffalo trails and Indian footpaths shared or commandeered by white European settlers on the march to find land.*

*…The latest "fashions"—woven from the coats of animals grazing peacefully just outside the back door.*

Erie Canal Locks

*...The closest doctor—a bit of family garden patch, nearby woods, or flora-filled banks of the local creek.*

*...And the only long-distance communications system—a mix of hope and fear: hope that nothing would befall the horse, and fear that the rider would find irresistible the temptations of the convenient crossroads taverns that lay in his path.*

Before the late eighteenth century, the country's earliest "infrastructure" was by and large a catch-as-catch-can affair, cobbled together by necessity, designed on a wing and prayer, and driven almost wholly by local needs. If something needed to be built, the job fell to whoever was handy—and could manage to lay their hands on a decent set of tools. Even the tools themselves were often jury-rigged affairs, put together with whatever wood, stone, metal and brawn could be mustered.

Roads ranked particularly high on the list of priorities. Especially coveted were post roads, for ensuring the (relatively) timely delivery of mail. The call for reliable delivery routes was so strong, in fact, that Section 8 of the U.S. Constitution commanded the fledgling federal government to take on the responsibility, ranking it higher on the list than declaring war, raising militia or fighting off pesky pirates.

As settlers fanned out from the coasts in search of land and opportunity, the demand for better (and less muddy) ways and means of travel was answered in part by the entrepreneurialism of private toll road builders who constructed thoroughfares and charged users a small amount for the privilege. State and local authorities also got into the act by authorizing roads and assigning upkeep to those who lived along the way—often to the loudly expressed annoyance of locals who felt they had better things to do than repair wash-outs to ease the transit of perfect strangers. Tavern owners were, of course, an exception: they welcomed the travelers with open arms.

The federal government joined in the road-building campaign. In 1803 Congress earmarked part of the proceeds from selling land in Ohio to finance the first few miles of the National Road.[i] Begun in 1811 at Cumberland, Maryland, the road was an impressive engineering feat for its day. The roadbed was 20 feet wide, and covered with a generous 18" helping of crushed stone. Rivers and creeks on the route were traversed by sturdy stone bridges. Many of the Conestoga wagons that carried settlers west to Ohio and points beyond during the first half of the nineteenth-century rocked, rattled and rolled over the 800-mile long Cumberland before dispersing to other points.

As the nation's agriculture-based economy began to be slowly but inexorably elbowed aside by the advent of the Industrial Revolution in the early nineteenth century, the newly-minted class of American industrialists poured money, energy and ingenuity into building canals—sometimes with the help of state money, but more often with private capital. In Connecticut, for example, the canal at Windsor Locks and the Farmington Canal were constructed almost completely by private enterprise. The 363-mile long Erie Canal, completed in 1825, was the brainchild of entrepreneur Jessie Hawley, but largely paid for and built by the state of New York. In the meantime, privately-financed steamboat lines plied the Mississippi, Great Lakes, and other waterways.

The mid-nineteenth century also ushered in the nation's rail network—a complex tale of transcontinental proportions and featuring a cast of characters whose accrual of major fortunes earned them the title of "robber barons" and transformed their last names into American business icons: Frick, Gould, Harriman, Huntington, Hill, Stanford, and Vanderbilt, among them. The federal government played a key supporting (and sometimes questionable) role by supplying land grants and pivotal financing to inspire completion of thousands of miles of track by chartered companies and private enterprise. Although the process of building the nation's huge rail network was frequently and deeply stained by violence, unabashed greed, abusive labor practices, sabotage, and more than a little political chicanery, it did have the desirable effect of supplying the nation with a large—and largely dependable—transportation infrastructure to link communities and markets coast to coast. In 1869, the year the transcontinental line was completed at Promontory Point, Utah, a trip from New York City to San Francisco required a mere 83 hours and 39 minutes, a far cry from the four uncomfortable weeks by wagon and water that had been the norm.

Not everyone greeted the new rail network with unbridled enthusiasm. Native Americans viewed the railroads as intruders and in violation of previously negotiated land treaties. "War parties" occasionally raided labor camps and killed workers; railroad management retaliated with security patrols and by hiring marksmen to kill buffalo, the Indians' primary food source.

The decades just before and after 1900 saw the steady proliferation of another major landscape feature: miles and miles of wire strung from building to building, pole to pole, town to town, and state to state. Telephone, telegraph, and electricity networks slowly crept across the country, tying together people and communities by supplying communications and power. Waterworks and dams also appeared, generally financed by local resources.

By and large the federal government's role in the wiring of the nation was one of regulatory nature rather than hands-on construction. As public concern about corporate and potential monopoly powers grew in the late nineteenth century, the federal government (as well as states) was nudged by popular outcry to adopt an oversight role, especially in the areas of utilities, railroads and other infrastructures considered vital to public life.[ii] The earliest antitrust legislation—The Sherman Antitrust Act—was passed in 1890. Its author, John Sherman, noted that "If we will not endure a king as political power, we should not endure a king over the production, transportation, and sale of any of the necessaries of life."

## THE COMMON DEFENSE

Providing for the "common defense" also fell to the federal government. The authors of the Constitution considered it such an important job that it was incorporated into the document's Preamble. At the time of the nation's formation, Congress authorized the Army to build or strengthen fixed harbor defenses. Fort Monroe, Virginia; Fort Washington, Maryland; and Fort McNair in Washington D.C. still stand as reminders of the nation's earliest "homeland defense." (That's not to say they were

**TIMELINE OF FEDERAL-LEVEL POLICYMAKING: 1775 – 1920**

**1775**—Creation of the Army, the Navy and the Marines

**1789**—Department of War created, along with Departments of State, and Treasury

**1790**—Creation of the Revenue Cutter Service, forefunner of the Coast Guard

**1798**—Aliens and Sedition Act passed in Congress as a collection of laws designed to control the activities of foreigners in the U.S.

**Early 19th Century**—Westward Expansion

**1803**—Louisiana Purchase

**1804**—Lewis & Clark expedition of Pacific Northwest funded by Army

**1849**—Department of Interior created, took over westward expansion activities from War Department

fool-proof: during the War of 1812, the British still managed to capture Washington and burn it.)

The Navy was authorized from the outset to construct "blue-water ships" to defend America's right to the sea lanes. *The U.S.S. Constitution,* at rest today in Boston Harbor, is an example of the ships of that era. The Coast Guard, formed in 1790 as the Revenue Cutter Service, maintained lighthouses, monitored ports and coastlines against smugglers and pirates, and did its best to collect federal revenues from shippers.

Westward expansion was another area in which the federal government played an important role. In addition to its sponsorship of such westward-ho infrastructure projects as the National Road, the government sent the U.S. Army to patrol wagon roads in the role of frontier "police." The Army built forts and supplied soldiers in the West throughout much of the nineteenth century, providing protection to settlers who encountered Native American resistance to white encroachment. Over time, as the frontier disappeared under the pressure of development, state and local institutions took over and the Army's role as protector diminished accordingly. The military played yet another role on home turf. . . until the law curtailed its power: During Reconstruction, federal soldiers occupied the South, protecting former slaves and making arrests as they saw fit—until passage of the Posse Comitatus Act in 1878 squelched the military's civilian law enforcement powers.[iii]

For much of the nation's first century, the small federal military appeared to be adequate to secure the nation's borders and frontier, at least during peacetime. Engagements tended to be isolated and small, notwithstanding notable exceptions such as Custer's Last Stand in 1876.

But the struggles that attended federal military mobilization for the Civil War in the 1860s, the Spanish-American War in 1898, and—espe-

**Late 18th Century and Early 19th Century—**
**Communication and Transport Systems**
US Postal Service played a significant role in the expansion of roads and modes of transportation. Postal employees regularly took their life into their hands by

trying to make postal service more efficient and faster.
1823—waterways are declared post roads
1831—railroads begin carrying mail for short distances
1838—railroads are declared post roads

cially—World War I exposed the lack of national-level "preparedness" for times of heightened peril.

In August 1914, for example, the Chief of Staff of the Army's Eastern Department at Governor's Island, New York, made a humble request to a colleague: "We are without European maps and without funds to buy them at this headquarters . . .You will probably have some maps at the War College from which you might send us a few. If so, please do so at once."[iv]

## PAINFUL LESSONS

As the nation slowly and reluctantly edged toward engagement in the European war, Congress included language in the Army's appropriations legislation in August 1916 to establish a Council of National Defense (CND) and related Advisory Committee to streamline industrial mobilization in support of defense—a first. CND membership consisted of six secretaries: War, Navy, Interior, Agriculture, Commerce, and Labor. The Advisory Committee's seven members included a college president, a leading railroad engineer, the president of Sears, the president of the American Federation of Labor, the head of the American College of Surgeons and stockbroker Bernard Baruch.[v]

Under the terms of the act, the Council was charged with the "coordination of industries and resources for the national security and welfare" and with the "creation of relations which render possible in time of need the immediate concentration and utilization of the resources of the Nation." But the snail's pace slowness with which the Board was constituted—six months—frustrated the Wilson White House and a fast-moving and more vigorous War Industries Board (under Bernard Baruch and peopled with more representatives from industry and the military) was set up.

TIMELINE OF FEDERAL-LEVEL POLICYMAKING: 1775 – 1920

**1862—Railroad Act** aided the construction of a railroad and telegraph line between Missouri and the Pacific Coast. Communications no longer had to be routed through Panama.

**1878—Posse Comitatus Act** passed making it a crime to use the military for domestic law enforcement in the U.S. under most circumstances.

The Council of National Defense remained active, breaking ground in another area: civil defense. Under the guidance of the CND, states and even localities organized their own Councils. As fear of invasion of U.S. soil slowly faded, the national "civil defense" program shifted focus from protecting home turf from physical threats to promoting initiatives to support troops overseas, quelling domestic dissension and pressuring U.S. citizens to support the war. Some of the activities were questionable, including enforcement of loyalty oaths, organizing boycotts of newspapers and magazines deemed unpatriotic, marking the residences of people suspected of disloyalty with yellow paint, and vigilante activity against German language publications. Other activities included bond drives, food and fuel conservation programs, and recruitment for the armed forces.[vi] Oklahoma alone claimed to have more than one million volunteers participating in local CND work.

The aches and pains of haphazard national preparedness during World War I were plentiful and eye-opening. The stumbling of the CND and the general lack of coordination in the government was frustrating to those both inside and outside the government. One result of the fumbling was especially stinging to the military: When the nation shed its official neutrality policy in the spring of 1917, the country's munitions industry was knee-deep in contracts to supply French and British troops.[vii] The American military was out of luck.

"World War I taught us that it was not enough to have an immense capability to produce large amounts of war materiel," suggests one analysis of the munitions debacle. "Effective planning had to accompany that capability. Large amounts of money were set aside to purchase much needed military hardware and orders were placed. However, due to the complete absence of mobilization plans, we fought the war by either bor-

**TIMELINE OF FEDERAL-LEVEL POLICYMAKING: 1775 – 1920**

**1903**—Militia Act increased the role of the state militias by training, organizing and equipping them according to Army standards. It also delegated them as a Reserve force for the U.S. Army.
**1916**—creation of the Council of National Defense as part of the Army Appropriations Act

**1917**—the United States joined the Allies in World War I (April)
**1917**—War Industries Board (July) created to coordinate industrial production for the war effort
**1920**—National Defense Act

# Shade of Gray: Defining Critical Infrastructures

**E**xecutive Order 13010, signed by President Bill Clinton on July 15, 1996, defined the term 'critical infrastructures' for the first time in official federal policy. The Executive Order states that critical infrastructures are systems that are "so vital that their incapacity or destruction would have a debilitating impact on the defense or economic security of the United States."[1]

At that time, eight sectors of critical infrastructure were identified: telecommunications; electrical power; gas and oil; banking and finance; transportation; water supply; emergency services; and continuation of government.

Since then, the definition of critical infrastructures has evolved[2] to include additional sectors that support public health, assure continuity of government services and maintain public confidence (such as the security of national monuments and special events).[3] Today, the official list of critical infrastructure sectors has expanded to fourteen and includes many subdivisions.[4]

The exercise in defining critical infrastructure is useful, but also limited. While providing a framework for thinking about and discussing critical infrastructure, it's important to note that not all sectors are created equal. Components of one infrastructure, for example, can differ markedly in their criticality to the survival of the overall system. A high degree of redundancy and a low number of interdependencies mean that disruption or failure would likely only cause a localized inconvenience, not a national catastrophe.[5] For example, the telecommunications sector is considered a critical infrastructure, yet there is a considerable amount of redundancy built into the sector. Disruptions can be bypassed while the system is under repair. At the same time, within the telecommunications network there exist critical nodes that underpin communications for millions of routine and mission critical functions.

A guiding rule of thumb suggested by the Congressional Research Service to weight criticality includes an infrastructure's vulnerabilities in terms of system redundancy, interdependencies and critical node location.[6] To the untrained eye, determining the true level of criticality is a difficult task. Even among experts lively disagreement abounds.

[1] Executive Order 13010, Federal Register, Vol. 61, No. 138, July 17, 1996

[2] See definitions for 'critical infrastructure' in the following documents: The Clinton Administration's Policy on Critical Infrastructure Protection: Presidential Decision Directive 63, White Paper, May 22, 1998; Defending America's Cyberspace: National Plan for Information Systems Protection. Version 1.0. An invitation to a Dialogue. White House 2000; Executive Order 13231, Federal Register, Vol. 86, No. 202, October 18, 2001

[3] Critical Infrastructures: What Makes an Infrastructure Critical?, John Moteff et. al., Congressional Research Service Order Code RL31556 (Updated January 29, 2003)

[4] http://www.dhs.gov/dhspublic/display?theme=73&content=1375

[5] Moteff et. al.

[6] Ibid, p. 12 - 13

rowing or buying guns, munitions, airplane and other material from the French and British."[viii]

President Woodrow Wilson, who effectively nationalized several industries for the course of the war, angering many of the nation's business elite in the process, spun the thriving American arms industry as "an arsenal of freedom." Others weren't so sure. Some blamed the arms traders for pushing the United States into the war after the sinking of the British liner Lusitania, which Germans torpedoed on the grounds that the ship was supposedly being used to transport American-made arms. One thousand people died, including many Americans.

During and after the war, public concern about the way the war had been handled brought calls for controls on the country's arms traders, who were dubbed "The Merchants of Death." A flurry of post-war Congressional investigations into war profiteering by many American businesses likewise heightened public dismay over the lack of planning that had seemingly allowed such excesses to take place.

That the country's arms industry was so strong, while the ability of the federal government to harness it was so inadequate, prompted calls for a serious post-war look at the military's organization. Leaders such as War Industries Board chairman Bernard Baruch were disturbed that the government had had to essentially commandeer such basic infrastructures as the shipping, railroad, telephone and telegraph industries to try to meet its needs on an emergency basis. Better planning was called for. Just after the war ended, Baruch urged creation of a peace-time skeleton organization based on the experience of the war-making agencies.

For better or worse, the nation emerged from the Great War with a war-forged and formidable industrial base, as well as a heightened awareness of the dangers of planning vulnerabilities and the value of preparedness.

The nation would have twenty years to absorb the lessons and make good on them before the next global conflict put it to the test.

[i] Today, Route 40 follows much of the original roadbed. Many of the original stone bridges remain.

[ii] Bill Harris, a Commissioner with the President's Commission on Critical Infrastructure Protection notes: "As the railroads developed they became all powerful. If railroad management had a falling out with a particular industry or a particular community and didn't put a track through that community or didn't provide service to that particular industry, they—the industry or community—were dead. We had to develop a whole set of regulatory authorities to rein in the otherwise unbridled power of the management of railroad companies." (Harris, William. Interview, George Mason University Critical Infrastructure Protection Oral History Project, 31 March 2004.)

[iii] A brief history of the U.S. Northern Command can be found at <http://www.northcom.mil/index.cfm?fuseaction=s.home_history>. Or search at <http://www.northcom.mil>.

[iv] Michael J. McCarthy, "Lafayette, We Are Here": The War College Division and American Military Planning for the AEF in World War I, M.A. thesis (Marshall University, May 1992) Chapter 2: 4 <http://medix.marshall.edu/~mccarthy/thesis/>.

[v] Baruch apparently preferred to call himself a speculator; the Wilson administration identified him as a banker. (John A. Dodds, "Bernard Baruch and the Founding Myth: War Industries Board," Tiger Times, October 2001, Vol. 76, Issue 7: 2 <http://www.ndu.edu/icaf/association/TTOCT01.pdf

[vi] Walter G. Green, III, ed., The Electronic Encyclopedia of Civil Defense and Emergency Management <www.richmond.edu/~wgreen/ECDnatdefcounI.html> and <http://www.richmond.edu/~wgreen/encyclopedia.htm>.

[vii] U. S. arms exports in 1916 alone were more than $1 billion. (<http://tri.army.mil/tsac/wwi.tm>.)

[viii] Michael J. Terry, "Mobilizing the Deteriorating Defense Industrial Base," 1990 <http://www.globalsecurity.org/military/library/report/1990/TMJ.htm>.

*"I should like to offer the hope that the shadow over the world might swiftly pass. I cannot. The facts compel my stating, with candor, that darker periods may lie ahead."*

President Franklin D. Roosevelt
September, 1939

Cabinet members watch with mixed emotions as President Franklin D. Roosevelt signs U.S. declaration of war against Japan at 4:10 pm on December 8, 1941.

# CHAPTER 2

# Building A New Foundation:

## The New Deal and World War II

*"I want to be as clear about this as I can....Everyone in this country—all of us—must face the fact that civil defense is, and will continue to be, just as vital to American security as our armed forces, our defense production and our aid to allies and friends abroad....Every weakness in our civil defense adds to the strength of a potential enemy's stockpile of atomic bombs...."*

President Harry S. Truman
April 1951

Like its predecessor, World War II tested the nation's preparedness structure and, at least initially, found it wanting. But not for lack of trying—between the wars—on the part of the War Department.

Determined to learn from the eye-opening and unsatisfactory mobilization experiences of World War I, Congress in the National Defense Act of 1920 assigned the Office of the Assistant Secretary of War the task of figuring out what had gone wrong and how to fix it so it wouldn't happen again. The War Department dug into the task, possibly driven as much by a desire not to be embarrassed again as by a genuine drive to show that it could grasp the complex nature of conducting modern warfare. After all, the nation had escaped having a global war land on its doorstep this time, but there were no guarantees that the next one might not be fought on home turf.[i]

No fewer than four distinct plans came out of the effort. In 1924, the first plan emerged. In three laborious volumes, it detailed what was essentially a military procurement plan. An industrial mobilization super agency was to be established either by the executive or legislative branch for the purpose of "coordinating, adjusting and conserving the available agencies for resources so as to promptly and adequately meet the maximum requirements of the military forces and the essential needs of the civilian population." The model was loosely based on the War Industries Board that Bernard Baruch had headed.

An unfortunate assumption in the plan—and in all subsequent plans except the final one—was that the United States would never begin war preparations before formally declaring war. War plans were predicated on the notion of an easily identified "M-Day," a single date on which mobilization and a declaration would happen simultaneously.

But the War Department had not yet grasped the fact that by the time a formal declaration was issued, the American arms industry would no doubt already be hard at work . . . supplying munitions elsewhere. The U.S. military would once again find itself at sixes and sevens, trying to arm and supply American troops. Furthermore, innovations in the mechanization of warfare had made long, drawn-out affairs more likely, a scenario that would require steady and protracted production of munitions and supplies.

"The pre-World War II concept of an M-Day plan in the safe to be pulled out and applied on the declaration of war is no longer tenable," said Alfred M. Hill, chairman of the National Security Resources Board in 1948. "It does not happen that the United States finds itself in a completely friendly and peaceful world and embarked on full mobilization the next day. Rather, what is needed is a process of continuous planning."[ii]

The 1930 and 1933 mobilization plans were equally unrealistic. The former offended sister federal agencies by giving them no role; the latter tripped itself up by stressing that "war is no longer simply a battle between armed forces in the field—it is a struggle in which each side strives to bring to bear against the enemy the coordinated power of every individual and every resource at its command"—a gung-ho sentiment at complete odds with the prevailing isolationist mood of the 1930s.

The 1933 plan also effectively placed the economy under military control—not an idea calculated to tickle anyone's fancy outside of the War Department. Nor was it likely to stir up fervor in a business community that was still stinging from charges of war profiteering, was deeply suspicious of New Deal programs, and viewed mobilization talk as a possible lead-in to a second helping of the strong arm tactics that some felt the Wilson administration had employed toward industry during World War I. That the mobilization plans were prepared by a military establishment with limited understanding of private enterprise only added to the private sector's skepticism.[iii]

The 1936 version of the industrial mobilization plan was essentially a revision of the 1933 effort, but failed to pass muster with economic guru Bernard Baruch, who was asked to review it. In a criticism of war planning that he would voice again and again, Baruch faulted the plan for not taking into account civilian needs. He also insisted that any industrial mobilization be carried out primarily under civilian, not military, control.[iv]

By the time the last interwar plan appeared, in 1939, the length of the effort had been reduced to a grand total of eighteen pages, a far cry from the three-volume 1924 saga. The brevity of the plan was perhaps a sign that a sense of futility had replaced fervor. An additional one hundred pages of "annexes," however, dealt with such infrastructure issues as power, fuel, transportation, and finance.

Although Roosevelt publicly rejected the plan and deemed its contents "secret," this time the military planners had gotten enough right that the President ultimately, if quietly, tapped parts of it for setting up some of the war agencies of World War II. For one thing, the naive M-Day scenario had been jettisoned; for another, the 1939 plan finally recognized a fundamental truth: the country's industry and infrastructure were inextricably linked to national defense.[v]

## NEW DEAL: NEW INFRASTRUCTURE

President Franklin D. Roosevelt, of course, had already come to that conclusion. By the time the 1939 plan was submitted—and rejected—mobilization for war had been quietly underway for several years. Although the politically savvy President knew better than to ignore the strong anti-war sentiments of the citizenry and Congress, he also knew that if the country dawdled too long before getting ready to join the war abroad, the war would simply find its way to America's doorstep.

New Deal programs designed to jumpstart the economy were tailor-made to ease the country toward preparedness. In 1934, a grant of $10 million from the Public Works Administration (PWA) was used to buy vehicles for the cash-strapped Army. In 1935, $100 million in PWA funds were earmarked for the War Department, two-thirds which was devoted to construction projects.

In 1937, after the Japanese attack on China and the bombing of a U.S. gunboat (the USS *Panay*), Roosevelt began quietly steering New Deal money toward projects to strengthen the nation's outlying defense network. The Hawaiian Works Progress Administration (WPA), for example, was moved under War Department control on April 1,1938, assuring the nervous military there that its projects would receive top priority. A 1959 history of mobilization during the war notes that: "Between 1935 and 1939 when regular appropriations for the armed forces were so meager, it as the WPA worker who saved many Army posts and Naval stations from literal obsolescence."[vi]

By mid-1940—as the war heated up in Europe—the Works Projects Administration (the name had changed in 1939) had disbursed $432 million in coordination with civilian and military sponsors to launch national defense-related projects, including highways, airports, bridges, rail mileage, harbors, and Navy yards.

The attack on Pearl Harbor in December 1941 swept away any remaining doubts about U.S. involvement in the war, as well as any Congressional obstacles to full-speed-ahead mobilization. The nation quickly scrambled to harness its industrial base and citizenry to an all-out effort to fight and win a war on two fronts.

"At home, Americans built railroads, roads, bridges, tunnels, ports, airfields, electrical power and fluid distribution systems, factories, arsenals, depots, shipyards, training centers, military bases, even towns and cities," notes a 1997 history of the World War II infrastructure push. "All this—focusing on speed of construction and speed of production—contributed to a vast new network of infrastructure which revised the correla-

---

**TIMELINE OF FEDERAL-LEVEL POLICYMAKING:** 1930s – 1950s

**1932—Civilian Conservation Corps** created 37 days after FDR's inauguration. The Corps was also known as Roosevelt's "Tree Army" and they were tasked with addressing the soil erosion and natural resource depletion problems of the West.

**1933—Public Works Administration** created as part of the National Industrial Recovery Act. A New Deal initiative of the FDR administration to build public works project as a means of creating employment. PWA was abolished in 1941.

tion of American labor, raw material, transport, and electric power across the land. The result was a far more extensive, cohesive, flexible and dynamic pattern of production than anything the world had previously known. It revolutionized the capital underpinnings of the American economy not only for war but also for the peace in the aftermath."[vii]

While American industry pumped out munitions and supplies, the Office of Civilian Defense (created on May 20, 1941 and headed by New York Mayor Fiorello LaGuardia) urged citizens to watch the skies, seas, and their next-door neighbors for signs of potential menace. The call echoed the program that the Council of National Defense had promoted during the previous global conflict—in essence, asking citizens to act as soldiers on the home front. Among the "official" roles that were available in civil defense in the infrastructure protection area were fire-watching, and assignments on road and utility repair crews. LaGuardia asked Americans to "give an hour a day for the U.S.A." By June 1943, 10 million Americans had volunteered for Office of Civilian Defense (OCD) duties.

Various departments of the fast-growing federal government redoubled their efforts to construct infrastructure that would serve immediate war purposes, and turn the central government into a major infrastructure-building machine. A few examples:

- The Petroleum Administration for War (construction of oil refineries)
- The Civil Aeronautics Administration (airports)
- The Federal Works Agency (civil infrastructure and community support)
- The Reconstruction Finance Corporation (especially its offshoot, the Defense Plant Corporation)
- The Veterans Administration (mainly hospitals)
- The National Housing Agency (housing for war workers and their fam-

## TIMELINE OF FEDERAL-LEVEL POLICYMAKING: 1930s – 1950s

**1933**—Tennessee Valley Authority Act signed by Roosevelt to initiate construction on one of the nation's biggest public works projects - to create a series of dams along the Tennessee River and its tributaries. In addition to improving navigability on the Tennessee River, irrigation of farm lands and increased flood control, the TVA also generated electricity and brought economic development to the rural farmers.

ilies through The Federal Home Loan Bank Administration, The Federal Housing Administration and The Federal Public Housing Authority)

- U.S. Maritime Commission (shipyard construction)
- The Bureau of Reclamation (dams)

One of the most impressive projects for sheer size and speed was construction of the Pentagon, the world's largest office building. Construction began in September 1941 and in sixteen months the four million square foot building was completed. Another even larger construction project entailed building three top-secret cities to the tune of $2 billion to accommodate workers involved in the Manhattan Project to build an atomic bomb.[viii]

## RESISTING "MISSION CREEP"

As the need for wartime construction and manufacturing escalated, so did calls for protection of nonmilitary facilities of all types. Before the United States entered the war, the War Department had sought in pre-war planning to limit its own responsibility for protecting nonmilitary installations, such as public works, utilities, and industrial plants. The campaign had plenty of precedent from the previous war, when similar calls for protection of civilian or state and local property had engulfed the tiny Army. In 1919, an exasperated Secretary of War Newton D. Baker had tried to enunciate a policy to preclude the diversion of soldiers to protect infrastructure: "The responsibility for the security of property, be it federal, state, municipal, private, rests first upon the local government, then upon state, and only devolves upon the Federal Government when all other forces of the locality or state have been exhausted or have been found insufficient to meet the emergency."[ix]

TIMELINE OF FEDERAL-LEVEL POLICYMAKING: 1930s — 1950s

1935—Works Progress Administration created as part of the Emergency Relief Act. It was designed to create jobs in the public sector for the unemployed. It was terminated in 1943.

1945—Office of Civil Defense is dismantled by Truman as the prospect of major military attack on North America diminished with the wind-down of WWII.

Baker might have had the Posse Comitatus Act of 1878 in mind when he insisted: "The true rule to be followed is that the public military power of the United States should in no case be substituted for ordinary police powers of the States, and should be called into service only when the state, having summoned its entire police power, is still unable to deal with the disaster which threatens it."[x]

Baker's declaration notwithstanding, the Army ended up doing the lion's share of infrastructure defense tasks in both world wars. The military had hoped that the trained civilians of the National Guard would be up to the job of protecting non-military facilities. But when National Guard members were inevitably pulled by necessity into official military duty, the states lost their only real source of strength for handling internal security tasks. Attempts to raise "home guards" as substitutes generally faltered because recruits often could only help out for short periods of time.

"There can be no argument as to the importance of protecting our plants against sabotage," said General George Marshall, during World War II. "But I am convinced that the use of soldier guards is expensive and not particularly expedient. In effect, we recognize this when we use civilian guards to protect War Department buildings which offer a problem in protection somewhat similar to that of industrial plants. If the War Department were to accept responsibility for guarding plants and installations, I anticipate an endless stream of requests from owners to obtain a detail of troops for their plants. Plainly, we could not afford such a diversion of our military effort."

General Joseph W. Stilwell jotted in his journal a similar frustration:

Requests for Army Guards: Terminal island, shipbuilding plants, commercial radio stations, railroad bridges and tunnels, railroad crossovers, dams, water supply, power plants, oil wells, tanks, and refineries. Aircraft manufacturing plants, hospitals, aqueducts, harbor defenses. . . .Everybody makes a case for his own installation, and nobody gives a damn if the Army bogs down and quits training.[xi]

Eventually a solution of sorts was found. Much of the protection accorded private property or public utilities was accomplished more or less satisfactorily by military police battalions and by Army oversight of civilian guards hired by private industry. The Army provided training and organized the guards in a way that put them under Army regulations for the duration of the conflict.

Infrastructure monitored by the MP battalions and guards included telegraph and telephone wires; wharves and docks; key bridges; government plants; storage depots; terminals; and government agencies. They also patrolled train stations and helped out with civilian evacuations during emergencies. One MP Battalion was based at Pier Number 90, guarding the Queen Mary, Queen Elizabeth, and three other cruise ships that were being used for troop transport. Guards discovered two bombs in the Queen Elizabeth's troop section. Other battalions monitored electrical installations and such critical transportation nodes as the Sault St. Marie Canals, through which approximately 90 percent of the nation's iron ore supply traveled.

As a cobbled-together solution, it worked, but a system that essentially called on the military to deputize civilian guards was far from ideal in the eyes of the nation's military leaders. In the future, the War Department (soon to be renamed Department of Defense) would continue mightily to resist a role in civilian defense that it felt to be a dangerous distraction—or "mission creep"—from its larger goal of keeping any and all conflicts from reaching U.S. shores in the first place.

Said Marshall bluntly: "It would be a mistake for the War Department to recede from the policy that the protection of plants and installations is the primary responsibility of operators, owners, and local and state governments."

## A NEW STRATEGY FOR NATIONAL SECURITY

By the time World War II ended, the federal government was a far cry from the small enterprise it had been for much of the first 150 years of the nation's history. Prior to the war, state and local governments together spent far more than the federal government. But from 1942 on, Washington's annual expenditures handily beat the combined spending of all state and local governments.[xii]

The nation was also now the world's major superpower, a gain in global stature that the Truman administration translated into a complete overhaul and upgrade of the nation's military and intelligence functions. In 1947, Congress passed the National Security Act, setting in motion one of the most important reorganizations in the history of the federal government—and setting up a governance structure that would remain largely intact for the next half century.

# The Defense Production Act of 1950

Congress enacted the Defense Production Act (DPA) in 1950 just as the Korean War was getting underway. The DPA authorized the President to prioritize and/or reallocate the industrial resource base in support of domestic defense and military readiness. Its intent was to ensure that goods and services would be delivered where they are most needed "to promote the national defense."[1] The main philosophy driving the DPA was—and remains—that industrial and technological superiority are key components of the larger defense strategy of projecting U.S. military power overseas.[2]

In the half century since the DPA was first enacted, it has gone through numerous reauthorizations and several lapses.[3] At the end of the Cold War, the threat environment was uncertain which led to congressional concern over the necessity of the DPA and its applicability to the new world order. Proposals for its modernization were submitted, but only small modifications were made.

In its 1997 final report, the President's Commission on Critical Infrastructure Protection recommended a reinvigoration of the DPA, as well as the addition of language to recognize critical infrastructures as "essential to national security." In 2003, the DPA was reauthorized and incorporated the PCCIP's recommendation.[4]

[1] Defense Production Act: Purpose and Scope, by David E. Lockwood, Congressional Research Service Order Code RS20587 (Updated October 16, 2002)
[2] Use of the Defense Production Act of 1950 for Critical Infrastructure Protection, by Lee M. Zeichner (September 2001)
[3] See Defense Production Act: Purpose and Scope for overview on the DPA's reauthorizations
[4] S. 1738, Defense Production Act Reauthorization of 2003

One thrust of the legislation was aimed at unifying the military by bringing the Army, Navy and newly created Air Force together under one roof in a new Department of Defense (DOD). The act also created the National Security Council (NSC), the National Security Resources Board (NSRB), the Munitions Board and the Research and Development Board. The new apparatus included the new Central Intelligence Agency, an outgrowth of the old Office of Strategic Services.

The overarching goal of the National Security Act was to institutionalize a method for coordinating foreign and defense policy, activities that had been carried out on a very informal basis by Roosevelt (and on an even more by-the-seat-of-the-pants basis by his predecessors.) Although Truman initially resisted calling on the National Security Council for advice,[xiii] his attitude shifted when the U.S.S.R. shocked the world by detonating an atomic bomb in August 1949, several years before many experts had predicted. When the Korean War ignited the following summer, peacetime suddenly didn't seem so peaceful.

In addition to overcoming his distaste for the NSC, Truman reversed his earlier decision to dismantle the federal-level civil defense program of World War II, launched on his predecessor's watch. As part of the administrative wind-down after the war, in 1946, he had signed Executive Order 9562, abolishing the Office of Civil Defense that Roosevelt had created in 1941.

As events in 1949 and 1950 unfolded and a crisis atmosphere enveloped Washington, Congress passed the Federal Civil Defense Act, providing statutory authority for a new civil defense effort—the Federal Civil Defense Administration. The FCDA, however, ran into trouble almost immediately.

Among other things, the civil defense program started its life having to swim upstream against the ever-growing determination of the Department of Defense to remain unencumbered by civilian concerns. DOD wanted to focus on a new grand strategy to assure an American presence everywhere in the world, to build up American military strength overseas—in effect, to project sufficient power abroad to assure that future wars would be fought anywhere but on American soil. Civil defense had no place in DOD's plans.

In public forums on civil defense issues, DOD steadfastly insisted that civil preparedness was properly the responsibility of the private sector, citizens and state and local governments. The position wasn't new, but it was

## TIMELINE OF FEDERAL-LEVEL POLICYMAKING: 1930s – 1950s

**1947**—National Security Act enacted, creating the modern-day Department of Defense. The War Department became the Department of the Army. The air unit was separated out from the Army and became the Air Force. The Navy and Marines were united under the Department of the Navy. The legislation also created the National Security Council in the White House as well as the Central Intelligence Agency.

voiced with particular fervor after the experience of World War II had left DOD exasperated by civilian demands. In a pre-emptive strike against reoccurrence of the influx of requests for military protection by the private sector, the DOD's Civil Defense Board's "Bull Report" in 1948 calmly, but repeatedly, stressed that "the major civil defense problems are not appropriately military responsibilities. Such problems are civilian in nature and should be solved by civilian organization." The country's military needed to be free "for their primary mission of operations against the enemy."

In 1950, a similar sentiment was expressed, albeit less formally, during Senate hearings that led to passage of the Federal Civil Defense Act. Asked to explain why DOD didn't want civil defense under its umbrella, Bull Board staff member Colonel Barnet W. Beers said simply: "The feeling in military circles . . .is that they have got enough to do as it is."[xiv]

The Federal Civil Defense Administration's status as an independent agency didn't help. Although the White House theoretically was to look out for its interest, Truman's low enthusiasm for civil defense—public statements to the contrary notwithstanding—left it without a larger, seasoned departmental sponsor to help it on Capitol Hill.[xv] The small civil defense effort would get off to a rough start for other reasons as well, including managerial missteps early on, Presidential ambivalence, Congressional skepticism and general uncertainty about the true scale and scope of the nuclear threat from the U.S.S.R.

A nagging question, too, involved money. Who should foot the bill? In a moment of deeply-regretted miscalculation, Millard Caldwell, the fledgling FCDA's administrator, suggested that a mind-boggling $300 billion would be needed to provide a nationwide system of deep shelters to protect the entire U.S. population. Although Caldwell had tossed out the number to describe an ideal system—not a realistic one—the figure stuck. The nascent program's credibility crashed and never fully recovered.

**TIMELINE OF FEDERAL-LEVEL POLICYMAKING: 1930s – 1950s**

**1949**—Creation of the Federal Civil Defense Administration in response to the Soviet detonation of its first nuclear device.
**1950**—Federal Civil Defense Act provided post facto statutory authority for the FCDA. FCDA became an independent agency. Until the legislation was repealed in 1994, the federal government's civil defense program changed names, missions and structure many times.

Time and again, civil defense budgets in the range of well under $1 billion were submitted; Congress would usually respond by slashing the request by 80 or 90 percent or more. It didn't help that FCDA staff never seemed to be able to provide justification for their figures.[xvi]

At the same time that the civil defense effort tried to get off the ground, the National Security Resources Board, one of the entities created by the National Security Act of 1947, took up its assigned tasks. One of its main ambitions was to create the kind of think-ahead planning systems that had been missing or quickly stitched together during the two world wars. In the same vein, Congress gave the nod to a vigorous program of peacetime stockpiling of critical materials and passed the Defense Production Act (DPA) in September 1950. [xvii] Major provisions of the DPA included establishment of a Defense Priorities System and a Defense Materials System that would allow the President to allocate scarce resources to sustain production of items considered most crucial to national security. Financial incentives supplied by Title III of the DPA helped to spur industry to focus on expanding capacity for critical and strategic materials and machine tools that would be needed in time of war. Aluminum production doubled and the mining and processing of such important materials as tungsten, columbium, tantalum, copper and nickel were started or expanded. The nation would not get caught short on the supply front, not if government planners had any say in the matter.

The National Security Resources Board, the Defense Production Act of 1950, and the Federal Civil Defense Administration would soon be joined by dozens of other planning exercises and entities as the federal government sought to capture lessons from World War II and prepare as best it could for a future that seemed—to some, anyway—fraught with any number of new and novel dangers.

TIMELINE OF FEDERAL-LEVEL POLICYMAKING: 1930s – 1950s

**1950**—Defense Production Act authored the President to prioritize and/or reallocate the industrial resource base to support homeland defense and military readiness. (See sidebar for more info on DPA)

**1952**—E.O. 10421 assigned federal agencies the task of working closely with industry to identify facilities vital to industrial mobilization in the event of war.

The striving toward a perpetual state of preparedness also respond-ed—nearly a half-century late—to an observation and admonition offered by Secretary of War Elihu Root, in 1902, before the Senate Committee on Military Affairs:

> Neither law nor custom places the preparation of plans for national defense in the hands of any particular officer or body of officers and what is everybody's business is nobody's business. . . .It has usually been because staff officers have been designated under the dictates of expediency, (because the) American character rises superior to system or rather absence of system, that disaster has been avoided.

---

ⁱ The War Department did implement one immediate planning improvement after the war. In 1921, it drew up the Harbord List, a roster of 28 minerals that had been in short supply during World War I.

ⁱⁱ Arthur M. Hill, National Security Resources Board (Washington: National War College, 6 June 1948) 7. Hill was chairman of the National Security Resources Board (NSRB). Note that he delivered his comments at the National War College in 1948, the year before the Russians set off their first atomic bomb. The shift from a "friendly and peaceful world" to a hostile one happened with a bit more speed than Hill predicted. Hill's agency, the NSRB, was also not destined to last. Between Truman's distaste for anything associated with the National Security Act of 1947, and the Department of Defense's displeasure with any serious industrial mobilization activities not under its command, the NSRB was abolished in 1953 and its duties shifted to the Office of Defense Mobilization in DOD. (Douglas T. Stuart, Organizing for National Security, Strategic Studies Institute, U.S. Army War College. (Carlisle, Pennsylvania: U.S. Army War College, November 2000) <http://carlisle-www.army.mil/usassi/welcome.htm>).

ⁱⁱⁱ From the website of the Industrial College of the Armed Forces: "The Industrial College of the Armed Forces (ICAF) has served the Nation for over 79 years, preparing military officers and civilian government officials for leadership and executive positions in the field of national security. Established in 1924 in the aftermath of America's mobi-lization difficulties in World War I, its predecessor, the Army Industrial College, focused on wartime procurement and mobilization procedures. Bernard M. Baruch, who was a prominent Wall Street speculator and Chairman of the War Industries Board, is regard-ed as one of the founding fathers. With a unique and defining mission, the Army Industrial College rapidly expanded. The College was closed during World War II and then re-opened two years later in 1943 in the Pentagon. Before World War II ended, senior Army officers, including General Dwight D. Eisenhower (graduate of the Army Industrial College class of 1933 and instructor at the College for four years), supported the concept of a joint war college. In 1946, the name of the College changed to the Industrial College of the Armed Forces." (National Defense University, May 2005 <httpp://www.ndu.edu/icaf/history/index.htm>).

ⁱᵛ Baruch repeated his sentiment many times over the years. In 1946, during Senate hearings on the Unification of the Armed Forces, 1946, he noted, perhaps with a touch of exasperation: "It seems to me essential and intelligent, as I have suggested on other occasions, that there be continued in time of peace the proved framework of an organization comparable to the War Production Board which shall be constantly available for a time of emergency, and which will draw on the store of experience, good will, production technique, research technique and planned cooperation between the armed forces on one hand and private industry on the other." (United States. Cong. Senate Committee on Naval Affairs. Hearings on Unification of the Armed Forces. 79th Congress, 2nd session. S. 2044. (Washington: GPO, 1946) 148-149).

[v] The first part of the 1939 War Department plan was titled "The Utilization of National Resources and the Mobilization of Industry in Time of Major War." Price control—formerly a major issue—was handled in a single sentence. (Louis C. Hunter, Economic Mobilization Studies: Economic Mobilization Planning and National Security (Washington: Industrial College of the Armed Forces, Education Division, May 1952, Publication No. R151) 9).

[vi] R. Elberton Smith, The Army and Economic Mobilization (Washington: Office of the Chief of Military History, Department of the Army, 1959).

[vii] Hugh Conway and James E. Toth, The Big "L": American Logistics in World War II. Chapter: Building Victory's Foundation. Alan Gropman, ed. (Washington: National Defense University Press, 1997) 196 <http://www.ibiblio.org/hyperwar/USA/BigL/.>

[viii] Conway 224.

[ix] Boyce Wayne Blanchard, American Civil Defense 1945-1975: the Evolution of Programs and Policies, diss., University of Virginia, 1980.

[x] Conn, Stetson, Rose C. Engleman and Byron Fairchild, Guarding the United States and Its Outposts. 1964 (Washington: Center for Military History, 2000, CMH Pub 4-2) 73. <http://www.army.mil/cmh/books/wwii/Guard-US/>.

[xi] Conn 77.

[xii] The First Measured Century, 2005 May <http://www.pbs.org/fmc/book/11government1.htm>.

[xiii] Truman supposedly felt that creation of the NSC was a criticism of his foreign policy aptitude. He attended only 10 of the first 55 meetings of the group, effectively guaranteeing that the principals would come to him individually to talk over issues. (<http://www.whitehouse.gov/nsc/history.html>).

[xiv] United States, Cong., Senate Armed Services Committee, Hearings on S. 4217 and S. 4219: 80.

Quoted in Charles Fairman, Relation Between Armed Forces and Civil Authority in a Postatomic Attack Situation (Washington: Industrial College of the Armed Forces, 6 May 1954, Publication No. L54-128) 6. In an introduction to speech on civil defense given by Beers at the National War College, his host referred to him as "Mr. Civil Defense." Beers was also involved in the Hopley Report, a contemporaneous review of civil defense.

[xv] The FCDA began life under the wing of the NSRB, but the Civil Defense Act of 1950 established it as an independent agency, separate from the Executive Branch.

[xvi] Blanchard 52-80 passim.

[xvii] For an interesting piece advocating use of the DPA for managing critical infrastructure service failures, see Lee M. Zeichner, "Use of the Defense Production Act of 1950 for Critical Infrastructure Protection," September 2001 <http://www7.nationalacademies.org/cstb/wp_cip_zeichner.pdf

# CHAPTER 3

# Peaks of Fear and Valleys of Apathy:
## Industry and Defense During the Cold War

*"It is . . . clear that no matter how crushing a blow we can strike in retaliation for an attack upon us, to permit our great centers of population and industry to lie exposed to the weapons of modern war is to invite both an attack and national catastrophe. Therefore, our whole civil defense effort needs both strengthening and modernizing."*

President Dwight D. Eisenhower
July 1956

When Harry Truman left office in 1953, he handed off a federal government that had been transformed in just twenty years from the small inward-looking institution of pre-Depression America to a large bureaucracy organized to take a leading role on the world stage. The drama that would dominate that stage for the next half century was the Cold War and the looming threat of nuclear war. The script called for a constant state of war-alert, and the U.S. government was ready to take the lead.

Industry was willing, too. Or at least some of it was. John Redmond of Koppers Company, Inc., a metals manufacturer, seemed to welcome the prospect of taking action. In 1957, he told a class of the Industrial College of the Armed Forces:

The need for industrial defense planning on this wide scale is comparatively new. In August 1945, the first atomic bomb was dropped, less than twelve years ago. However, it was not until the time of the Korean incident that there was much real interest in any phase of the defense problems forced on humanity by the possibility of nuclear attack. In my opinion, tremendous progress has been made in accepting the problem for what it is and in getting something done in the way of planning.[i]

Indeed, planning would be a major preoccupation of both government and industry for the foreseeable future. The era of professional managers was in full flower and the development of programs a national passion.

The first priority was to build up the nation's military establishment to a level of strength and readiness that would make it a formidable factor in all future foreign policy matters. The federal establishment as a whole was to get behind the effort, supported by a war-tested industrial base.

"[I]n the atomic age, [the government] must maintain a posture of flexibility not experienced or even required in other wars," declared William E. Haines, Assistant Deputy Administrator of the Business and Defense Services Administration (BDSA) in the Department of Commerce, in 1955. "It must be ready at all times to obtain and assess attack damage information—rapidly and accurately. It must be prepared to shift overnight the emphasis and requirements for whole programs. It must be prepared to cope with a whole new set of production problems and difficulties that would make the War Resources Board mission in World War II seem almost like a war game. And in an atomic war, where the homeland is certain to be a battleground, it must deal with the new and staggering problems involved in the continuity, conversion, and recuperation of essential production and defense-supporting facilities, and countless subsidiary problems."[ii]

The government, however, could not do it alone, noted Haines. In language reminiscent of a call to arms, he went on to explain industry's role:

We in BDSA believe that an important part of the job of war production planning rests with the owners and managers of the Nation's great industrial enterprises. For it is in their laboratories and workshops where many of the incredibly efficient munitions of war are engineered and made. And [this] will probably be true to a far greater extent in an atomic war than it was in World War II, when it soon became apparent that our homes and factories would not become the objects of direct attack. It is our job in Commerce to stimulate industry to face up to new and great responsibility of management. That job is complicated by the shifting sands of day-to-day world tensions, particularly in this fiercely competitive period when businessmen prefer to devote themselves to current production problems rather than lay plans for an awful day that might never come.[iii]

In short, industry was no longer merely a supplier or vendor, but an integral part of the nation's security. And one that would probably need to be exhorted to do its part. Said Haines: "We cannot develop a sound program of industrial defense by alternating between peaks of fear and valleys of apathy."

Haines went on to describe some of the ways in which the BDSA was "working closely with the top managements of highly important companies in an effort to stimulate them to prepare" plans for "continuity of management, continuity of production, and facilities protection." Safeguarding records was emphasized, in a way that seemed slightly macabre: "Even though the plant itself may be lost, the surviving management, down to the supervisory level, should have a legacy of corporate knowledge available to them."

Some of the companies that had heeded BDSA's call included AT&T; Standard Oil; Consolidated Edison; U.S. Steel; Jones and Laughlin Steel; and, of course, Koppers, run by General Brehon Somervell.

Industries had also come together to develop plans for survival, presumably by helping each other within (or perhaps without?) the constraints of antitrust and instinctual competitiveness. Electronics, copper, iron and steel, chemical and 'allied' industries, petroleum and life insurance all had plans under development or in place by 1957.

## TIMELINE OF FEDERAL-LEVEL POLICYMAKING: 1956 – 1979

**1956**—Federal Aid Highway Act led to the construction of the modern day interstate system (See Sidebar on Interstate system)

**1958**—Reorganization Plan #1 consolidated the Federal Civil Defense Agency and the Office of Defense Mobilization into a single agency: Office of Civil and Defense Mobilization, located in the Executive Office of the President.

**1958**—Federal Civil Defense Act amended to provide federal funding for civil emergency preparedness.

"Protective construction" was another concept heavily promoted by industrial mobilization forces. Not only BDSA, but also some of the many other parts of the government concerned with industrial mobilization got into the act. The Defense Department's Office of Defense Mobilization put out a manual titled "Protective Construction for Industrial Facilities" DMO VI-4 (March 16, 1954) Another offering was "Standards for Plant Protection" by the U.S. Munitions Board. Both manuals included steps to prevent sabotage as one element in a multi-faceted effort to enhance continuity of operation.

Companies were also encouraged to make arrangements in advance for alternate production sources in dispersed sites, and stockpiling (at "safe locations") raw materials, components, end items, and maintenance and repair equipment, including key items of long lead-time production equipment.

Undertaking "advance construction planning" with an eye toward rebuilding as fast as possible after an attack was also promoted. "Currently, more than 30 key industries are at work on this problem through task groups composed of top-management representatives from the industry called together by the Department of Commerce, working through the Industry Advisory Committee machinery," a 1957 report noted. Industries that were busy stowing away blueprints (presumably at an off-site location) were steel, chemical, photographic film, machine tool, jeweled watch movement, rubber, and aluminum.

The chemical industry's plan, for example, took into account plant protection, reconstruction planning, management and company-wide planning, risk approval, continuity of management, protection of current assets (including dispersing bank accounts), protection of records, plant-level emergency and disaster planning. The group had also generated suggestions for proper design and lay-out in construction or revision and

TIMELINE OF FEDERAL-LEVEL POLICYMAKING: 1956 – 1979

1961—President Kennedy separated civil defense and emergency preparedness in to two separate agencies. Civil defense went to the Office of Civil Defense at the Department of Defense and emergency preparedness programs went to a new agency, Office of Emergency Planning (renamed the Office of Emergency Preparedness in 1968.)
1962—Cuban Missile Crisis led to a temporary surge in funding for shelter programs at the request of the Department of Defense.

expansion of existing plants to minimize bomb damage.

The same report noted mysteriously that "One very important and major industry has developed full-scale plans for transfer of production of their most vital defense product from vulnerably located facilities to existing facilities at dispersed sites in the event of attack damage." Within ninety days after an attack, the industry would expect to be up to almost full output.

Even entire business communities, bound by geography, got into the act. The businessmen of the San Francisco Bay area made a study of the problems their city would face in the event of a nuclear attack. The result, with the assistance of the Stanford Research Institute, was "The Community Plan for Industrial Survival."

## "GAMBLING ON BOMBING ODDS"

Clearly, the BDSA was busy. The organization had been established in October 1953 by President Dwight Eisenhower to replace the National Production Administration (NPA) launched by Truman in 1950 during the frenzy that accompanied partial mobilization for the Korean War. The agency was given the role of handling all of the defense and mobilization planning assigned to the Department of Commerce by the Defense Production Act of 1950, the National Security Act of 1947 and earlier defense stockpiling authorizations. Many activities related to industrial mobilization that DOD wasn't inclined to handle landed in Commerce, often at the door of the BDSA. So varied and numerous were its charges that an entire chapter could be devoted to its activities alone. One of its primary administrators, Thomas W. S. Davis told a class at the Industrial College of the Armed Forces:

> Since the very outset of mobilization for defense efforts, more fingers of responsibility for their successful promotion have been pointed at the Department of Commerce than any other agency. By the President and by the Congress, vital and indispensable duties have been heaped upon this Department and our 15 main offices and bureaus. These assignments to perform emergency functions, however, I'm happy to tell you did not catch us unaware or unprepared.[iv]

One of the higher profile activities in which the BDSA had a hand was an interagency group, the Industry Evaluation Board (IEB), the membership of which included an array of agencies whose missions or

# Paving the Way: The National Interstate Highway System

In the late 1930s, the Roosevelt administration recognized the economic and strategic military value of building a modern national highway system to supplement state and local roads. In 1938, a Federal Aid Highway Act was passed, but the outbreak of war prevented further action. The Act was passed again in 1944, 1952, 1954 and finally in 1956.[1]

Each incarnation of the bill addressed political and financial stumbling blocks. Issues ranged from the right balance of rural area versus urban area highway needs, to criteria for apportionment of highways by state (by population density vs. land distance/area), to cost sharing between states and the federal government.

President Dwight D. Eisenhower's enthusiasm was a critical factor in getting the final bill passed. In 1919, then Lt. Colonel Eisenhower had accompanied a military convoy that crossed the country from Washington, DC to San Francisco on bumpy, inadequate roads. During World War II, Eisenhower, by then a General, had taken note of the well-built German autobahn and its role in facilitating quick movement of German military and the Allied Forces.[2]

In the final version of the 1956 bill, federal assistance was earmarked for 90% of cost, up from nothing in the 1938 bill. Construction of the giant transcontinental system finally got underway after nearly two decades of debate. Although most people today refer to the system simply as "The Interstate," one of its official names is the National Interstate Defense Highway, a reflection of Eisenhower's vision of the system's importance for military transport and evacuation channels in the event of a nuclear attack.

[1] Weingroff, Richard F. "Federal Highway Act of 1956: Creating the Interstate System," Public Roads Online, U.S. Department of Transportation Federal Highway Administration, Vol. 60. No. 1, Summer 1996. Found at: www.tfhrc.gov/pubrds/summer96/p96su10.htm

[2] "National Defense Highway System," at www.globalsecurity.org/military/facility/ndhs/htm

constituencies touched on industrial mobilization planning.

The (IEB) had entered life by way of the National Security Council, was soon folded into Commerce, and provided "policy guidance" by DOD's Office of Defense Mobilization, which had taken over the National Security Resources Board's duties in 1953. The IEB had as a primary focus the challenge of identifying and rating thousands of products based on how important they might prove to be during war. Part of its authority for doing so came from Executive Order 10421 issued in 1952 (Truman), which laid out the national policy to ensure that "current and emergent physical threats" to the defense mobilization base "are adequately considered in planning preparedness programs and response mechanisms."

Besides its product-rating duties, the IEB was responsible for a Critical Industrial Facilities List, composed of all the industrial plants around the nation that had been identified as essential. This "mother of all lists," created with input from all relevant agencies, was used for "facility security purposes and related programs." As of 1957, the IEB had reviewed 5,000 facilities and generated ratings for 7,000 products. Described as the "one authoritative source in the executive branch of Government for the identification of essential products, services and facilities," the CIF List was—no surprise—also classified "secret."

Noted one contemporary report: "A knowledge of the irreducible core of essential industries and their producing facilities is so basic and so vital to the defense of the United States, that the determinations and evaluations of the Board (IEB), though subject to very high security safeguards, are distributed through the authority of the Director of the ODM to such officials through out the Government as must have them for various uses."v

The list came with one important caveat: "The work of the IEB, however, can never be 100 percent complete. There are constant changes in the industrial production pattern of the United States because of continuing improvements and expansions, changing military requirements, the completion of new producing facilities, scientific and technological changes in manufacturing procedures and the development of new products."

The list of IEB-identified facilities was integrated into the Office of Defense Mobilization's National Damage Assessment Program and included in its "magnetic tape records for analysis by means of high-speed computers." The list apparently also came in handy in BDSA's overall Industrial Defense Program, a joint effort of the government and industry. At least fifteen "basic defense" programs around the government also made use of the ratings and lists generated by the IEB, including programs devoted to stockpiling, civil defense, production expansion, damage assessment, "countersubversive activities," and "industrial and counterindustrial intelligence." The Executive Order that gave rise to the IEB also permitted the Continuity of Industry Division in the Office of Defense Mobilization (in DOD) to tap into the "expert knowledge available in Government agencies in discharging its mission of reviewing and approving analyses of products and facilities, and recommending security ratings of specific plants to the Secretary of Commerce."

Section 7 of the same Executive Order highlighted the responsibilities of private sector and the state and local government for physical security of critical facilities. Suggested measures included installation of fences, lights, positive entry control and identification systems, and intrusion alarms. The federal government was obliged only to "assure a standard minimum level of physical protection in those facilities that are most important to defense mobilization." Federal agencies with direct responsibility for "overseeing the industrial mobilization base" were to develop security standards and "provide advice, supervision and appraisal to industrial owners and operators to assure that physical security measures were satisfactorily incorporated into critical private sector facilities."

Another ambitious, but marginally successful initiative in plant security was the policy of encouraging "industrial dispersal" to reduce the concentration of critical industries in certain geographic locations. During WWII, the Allies had noted that Japan and Germany had both made an effort to decentralize portions of their industrial bases, to make destruction more difficult.

Announced officially by Truman in 1951, the dispersal program had been under development for at least three years. The plan was to use "to the greatest extent practicable" emergency loans, accelerated amortization, and the lure of special access to hard-to-get construction materials to entice key industries to relocate or open new plants in locations away from what had become highly concentrated industrial belts.[vi]

The National Security Resources Board (NSRB) was assigned the task of promoting the idea, but its outspoken chairman Arthur M. Hill made no bones about the fact that "it is utterly impractical to approach this problem from the standpoint of trying to relocate the existing industrial plants of the country or of trying to break up the concentration of the steel industry in Pittsburgh.[vii] Probably the best that can be done is to influence the location of new and replacement plants to secure some degree of protection through dispersion.[viii]

The Federal Civil Defense Administration had developed a list of likely target areas[ix], upon which the NSRB based its dispersal criteria. The NSRB used the then-popular assumption that nuclear damage would be limited to a three-mile zone from the point of impact. New facilities approved by the program were to be located ten or more miles from highly industrialized or densely populated sections or from major military installations, a distance that would soon be shown by nuclear fall-out results to be too close for comfort.

By 1953—when the NSRB's duties were absorbed into the Office of Defense Mobilization in DOD—some ninety industrial dispersion committees in major metropolitan areas served as local advisors to industry seeking dispersed sites. In the first six months of the same year, 84 percent of facilities costing 1 million dollars or more for which rapid tax amortization was granted were to be located on dispersed sites.

But the momentum was not destined to last. The wind-down of the Korean War helped to ease the urgency that had galvanized the initial push. The imperatives of the bottom line also soon took their toll. City governments became concerned about the hit to their tax bases if industries moved away or chose other expansion locations. And companies apparently didn't find the financial enticements offered by the government sufficient to offset the long-term costs of going where no company had gone before. The dispersal idea perhaps failed to take into account that a plant of any meaningful size couldn't simply emerge from the landscape without infrastructure to sustain it—not a small consideration to manufacturing interests that depended on a steady and large supply of fuel and electricity to keep production lines running.

Concern for the viability of supporting systems actually applied equally well to any "continuity of industry" program, whether dispersal or reconstitution after an attack. "It is also pertinent to recognize that though a given plant or other facility may survive but is without utilities or operators, it is useless until these elements are again made available," noted a 1956 study. "Therefore, in view of the high cost of protective construction, it is essential to plan for all elements—plant, utilities, materials, and per-

**TIMELINE OF FEDERAL-LEVEL POLICYMAKING: 1956 – 1979**

**1963**—National Communications System created to improve and monitor the telecommunication system to make it robust and resilient. The NCS would ensure national security communications, particularly during an emergency or crises.

**1974**—Disaster Relief Act made federal resources available pending a declaration by the President of a state of emergency. Disaster relief was addressed again in 1988 in the Stafford Act.

sonnel—in order to protect adequately against a producing entity. Less than this is sheer gambling on bombing odds."

Although the federal government put in place a number of programs designed to help the industrial base enthusiastically embrace its new role on the "front line," the clear message behind every initiative was that the ultimate responsibility for security lay with the private sector, not with the government:

> "Plant security, I need hardly remind the Industrial College, would be a major concern in war production," stressed Charles Fairman, a law professor at Washington University, in a 1954 guest lecture, "It is a responsibility definitely fixed upon management. But the civil authorities and the military authorities are vitally concerned in seeing to it that that responsibility is discharged."[x]

Similar sentiments were expressed by the Report of the Director of the Office of Defense Mobilization a year earlier: "It would require only a few of the new and terrible bombs to cause millions of casualties and disrupt essential defense industry. Our cities cannot be made invulnerable, but their chances of continuing as production centers must be greatly improved. The foundation is, of course, our military defense, which is being strengthened, including the development of an early warning system. In step with the improvement of our military defense, it is of primary importance that non-military defense measures be taken by industries and communities to protect themselves."[xi]

## AN UNCOMFORTABLE SUBJECT: CIVIL DEFENSE

While industry tried to perfect its "defense measures," communities grappled with a stickier wicket: civil defense. The effort, launched under Truman in 1949 and formalized by Congress in 1950, spent much of the 1950s stumbling along, haunting the halls of Congress and the Eisenhower White House looking for meaningful support. FCDA director Millard Caldwell's breathtaking blunder—the $300 billion price tag for deep shelters—had dug a very deep political hole for the agency from the get-go, one from which it never quite managed to climb its way back up to the light.

Civil defense's difficulties weren't particularly surprising. The specter of nuclear holocaust was so unpleasant, yet so powerful, that any discussion of it was bound to bring out strong emotions on every side.

Discussing the statistics of stockpiles, emergency loans for industrial dispersal, "protective construction," and a hundred other antiseptic-sounding measures for industrial defense was a piece of cake compared to talking about millions of dead or dying from direct blasts or fall-out effects.

In a sense, civil defense throughout the Cold War suffered from a variation on the NIMBY (Not in my backyard) syndrome. No one wanted to talk about it. No one wanted to pay for it. No one wanted to think it would ever really be needed. And probably fewer than were willing to admit it in public thought it would work.[xii] (Notable exceptions being Rand Corporation and Herman Kahn, who was perfectly willing to "think the unthinkable" and suggest that nuclear war might, in fact, not be so bad after all.[xiii])

Still, something needed to be done, if only to give Americans some sense of comfort, and the Russians the impression—even if false—that the U.S. was well-prepared to go underground if necessary to come out the winner in any showdown. Civil defense, such as it was, soon became a political card in the wary face-off between the two superpowers.

Much of the power of that card lay in the state of weapons delivery at any given time. As developments upped the ante or lessened the level of perceived threat, each country's alleged level of civil preparedness could be used to convince the other side that it had gained little advantage.

During the late 1940s and early 1950s, for example, the delivery of a nuclear device had been possible only by using relatively slow-moving bombers, which allowed several hours' notice. In 1957, the development of Intercontinental Ballistic Missiles cut delivery time dramatically—to approximately three hours—and then could be stopped only if detected with the 'sky-searching' capabilities of NORAD. In turn, the advent of satellite technology (Sputnik 1958) and later refinements bolstered sky-based espionage, reconnaissance and detection, both for offensive and defensive purposes. Not every countermeasure was a success: the much-touted Semi-Automatic Ground Environment (SAGE) system of computerized air defense cost billions of dollars but was obsolete by the time it was operational in 1961.

In Congress, proponents and detractors of civil defense fought over both the symbol and substance of the program, while DOD did its best to keep it at more than arm's length, maintaining a posture that one former general, Otto L. Nelson, Jr., termed the "polite but aloof position that civil defense is not their responsibility."[xiv] While their elected representatives duked it out, and DOD looked the other way, Americans were taught air raid drills (epitomized by the now much-lampooned "Duck and Cover" campaigns) and urged (on and off) to build home shelters and otherwise prepare for self-survival.

The civil defense program quickly became bound up in an emotional national debate over the "tipping point" at which prudent preparedness (in the guise of shelters and evacuation plans) edges toward imprudent provocation. ("Build it and they will come . . .mushroom clouds in tow.") The program became a political football, kicked around by those who considered civil defense "defeatism," Pollyanna-ish, strictly a state or local responsibility, or simply a silly waste of public money, energy and resources. It didn't help that a couple of powerful House members— Clarence Cannon and Albert Thomas—spoke loudly against the federal government being involved in civil defense at all. In spite of periodic breast beating in Congress, annual appropriations for U.S. civil defense programs never totaled much more than $1 billion (under Kennedy, in 1962) and, from 1952 to 1986, was never more than half that amount.

Civil defense's cause was not helped by White House ambivalence. Although each President of the period made public statements in support of civil defense, their actions (in the form of minimal appropriations requests) often belied their words. Changes in administrations every few years brought a roller-coaster of hot and cold support for meaty civil defense.

Truman set things in motion, for example, but wouldn't come to the tiny FCDA's rescue when it stumbled initially in Congress. Tight-fisted Eisenhower refused to initiate the fallout shelter program proposed by the agency, preferring the lower-cost evacuation concept instead.[xv] Even then, ever budget-conscious—he was lukewarm about financing it. But to his credit he was responsible for getting one piece of long-delayed infra-

TIMELINE OF FEDERAL-LEVEL POLICYMAKING: 1956 – 1979

1979—Creation of Federal Emergency Management Agency (FEMA) by consolidating all of the federal government's emergency and disaster management programs under one roof. The consoli-dation was plagued by interagency politics and power struggles within FEMA.

structure underway on his watch: the interstate highway system.

In 1961, Kennedy stirred things up with a speech after the Berlin Crisis that provoked a frenzy of home shelter building. He was apparently so dismayed by the hysteria that he never mentioned shelters in public speeches again.[xvi] Johnson, preoccupied with the Vietnam conflict and the civil rights movement, ignored civil defense as best he could. And Nixon made motions to invigorate the program but didn't back up his words with enough budgetary muscle to make a difference.

While the two nuclear superpowers poured billions of dollars into building massive nuclear stockpiles and civil defense struggled to get political traction, the scale and pace of the arms race began to raise ticklish questions in the minds of many Americans: Was survival of a nuclear exchange really possible? And, more to the point, was it even desirable?

Citizens and policymakers alike began to fret aloud that a "Bring it on!" mentality—manifested by the existence of millions of shelters—would make nuclear war not only thinkable but inevitable. By the 1970s, confidence in the nation's civil defense program had waned almost to the point of extinction. Beginning with Nixon—especially in the wake of 1972's historic ABM treaty with the U.S.S.R.—civil defense was still accorded lip service, but was quietly elbowed aside to make more room for "emergency preparedness" focused on recovery not from Russian nuclear attacks, but from Mother Nature's formidable force. The program shifted to a dual-use philosophy that was put to work on disasters caused by floods, hurricanes, tornadoes…as well as hazardous materials accidents.

Under Ford, the program briefly reemphasized nuclear preparedness, but by the time Jimmy Carter stepped into the White House, the end of civil defense as a serious national ambition was in sight. The consolidation of all preparedness-related programs into the Federal Emergency Management Agency in 1979 effectively pushed civil preparedness offstage.

By the time FEMA was formed, other vestiges of the early Cold War planning push had fallen by the wayside or otherwise lost their potency. The Defense Production Act was still on the books, but basically unused. The once-powerful Industrial Evaluation Board had all but stopped meeting. Many of the supplies in the country's nuclear fall-out shelters were forgotten. More than half of the nation's official defense stockpiles had been sold off between 1964 and 1976.

One explanation was simply human nature at work: complacency in the face of no imminent threat. Another big factor was fatigue. American industry had wearied of being asked, in the name of patriotic duty, to pour money and energy into a peacetime preparedness program that had a big price tag, but little day-to-day benefit. Perhaps most telling, business was tired of feeling that "their concerns and ideas for industrial mobilization and preparedness [had] been ignored or buried in government reports resulting in no action, no progress and a continuing deterioration of the industrial base," reported one survey of CEOs in 1981. "Among those organizations familiar with the history and planning for industrial preparedness the predominant opinions reflect a 'Quit studying the problem and get on with solving it' attitude."[xvii]

The "peaks of fear" that had marked the 1950s and early Cold War had by the 1970s more or less descended into "valleys of apathy." The long and largely uninterrupted peacetime expansion of the U.S. economy after the Korean War had whetted industry's appetite to focus on business profits, not government process. Washington's penchant for studying, studying, studying, had taken its toll. In spite of voicing "very grave doubts" about the condition of the nation's industrial base and transportation networks, by the beginning of the go-go decade of the 1980s, American industry had already turned its collective attention from a theoretical role as the nation's "front line" to the more tangible rewards of the bottom line. [xviii]

---

[i] John Redmond, Industry Planning for Continuity of Production (Washington: Industrial College of the Armed Forces, 28 February 1957, Publication No. L57-121).

[ii] William E. Haines, Planning for War Production (Washington: Industrial College of the Armed Forces, 27 January 1955, Publication No. L55-89).

[iii] Another speaker at the Industrial College of the Armed Forces echoed Haines's grim-but-determined outlook. Ted Enter, Director, Continuity of Industry Division, Office of Defense Mobilization: "It is fairly evident that our industrial centers will be prime targets. Having twice attained victory in war through the mobilization of our industrial might, it is reasonable to assume that an enemy would attempt to destroy or immobilize this potential, if possible, at the outset of the hostilities. Therefore, we may further assume that our industrial centers will become "frontline" targets and that, for the first time in our history, industry may be faced with the problem of production while under attack." (Ted E. Enter, Planning for Wartime Production, Washington: Industrial College of the Armed Forces, 8 February 1954, Publication No. L54-91).

[iv] Thomas W. S. Davis, Assistant Secretary of Commerce for Domestic Affairs, Role of the Department of Commerce in Economic Mobilization (Washington: Industrial College of the Armed Forces, 20 May 1952).

[v] C. F. Muncy, Governmental Organization for Industrial Production Planning for National Emergency or Mobilization. (Washington: Industrial College of the Armed Forces, September 1958, Publication No. R211) 26.

[vi] Ted E. Enter, Continuity of Industry Division, Office of Defense Mobilization, noted that "71 percent of our industrial capacity and 54 percent of our industrial workers are located in 50 of our metropolitan areas" and "The economic patterns of industry in the past many years have necessarily developed concentrations of industry capacity not only for purely economic reasons but also in considerable extent due to the interdependency of production." (Enter, 28 February 1954).

[vii] Accomplished quite effectively in the 1980s by economic forces.

[viii] Arthur M. Hill, National Security Resources Board (Washington: National War College, 6 June 1948) 9.

[ix] Available in a handy list titled Target Areas for Civil Defense Purposes, published in 1954

[x] Charles Fairman, Relation Between Armed Forces and Civil Authority in a Postatomic Attack Situation (Washington: Industrial College of the Armed Forces, 6 May 1954, Publication No. L54-128) 7.

[xi] L. A Appley, A Report to the Director of the Office of Defense Mobilization by the Committee on Manpower Resources for National Security: Manpower Resources for National Security (Washington: GPO, 18 December 1953, HD 5723 A 47) 70.

[xii] Charles Fairman, during his guest lecture at the Industrial College of the Armed Forces on May 6, 1954, noted with a touch of both humor and realism: "In the event of enemy action within domestic territory, disorganized civilians and organized evacuations would crowd the highways. The Armed Forces would be using the highways too. How should these movements be coordinated and controlled? It is no solution simply to say, shove the civilians into the ditch and let the troops go by. We must work out something much better than that." (Fairman 3.)

[xiii] Herman Kahn was the model for Dr. Strangelove in the Stanley Kubrick film of that name. Kahn authored "On Thermonuclear War (1960) and "Thinking about the Unthinkable" (1962). In 1977, Zbigniew Brzezinskii, told the Washington Post that "the fact of the matter is that if we used all our nuclear weapons and the Russians used all of their nuclear weapons, about 10 percent of humanity would be killed. Now this is a disaster beyond the range of human comprehension. It's a disaster which is not morally justifiable in whatever fashion. But descriptively and analytically, it's not the end of humanity." (Washington Post, 9 October 1977).

[xiv] The Department of Defense (DOD) was home to the nation's civil defense program from 1961 to 1972, but the Department managed to demote it sufficiently in the department's hierarchy to keep it from being either especially effective or terribly distracting.

[xv] Note, however, that it was at the end of Eisenhower's term that the ultra-secret, not to mention spacious, bomb shelter for federal leaders was constructed at the Greenbrier Resort in White Sulphur Springs, West Virginia.

[xvi] Kennedy delivered one of his most memorable lines about nuclear war to the United Nations General Assembly in September 1961: "Every man, woman, and child lives under a nuclear sword of Damocles, hanging by the slenderest of threads, capable of being cut at any moment by accident, miscalculation or madness."

[xvii] Harrison Fox and Stan Glod, faculty advisors, Industrial Preparedness Planning, Legislation and Policy, a class project for the Mobilization Studies Program, Industrial College of the Armed Forces (1981) 7.

# CHAPTER 4

# Under the Radar:

## New Threats, New Vulnerabilities in a Post Cold War World

*"We have not inherited an easy world. If developments like the Industrial Revolution, which began here in England, and the gifts of science and technology have made life much easier for us, they have also made it more dangerous. There are threats now to our freedom, indeed to our very existence, that other generations could never even have imagined."*

President Ronald W. Reagan
June, 1982, London

After several years of relative stability, or détente, between the two superpowers, the arms race regained momentum briefly under President Ronald Reagan (1980-1988). During the 1980s, the two superpowers came closer to confrontation than at any time since the Cuban missile crisis in 1962. Tensions began to mount in 1979, just before Reagan took office, when the Soviets invaded Afghanistan, a move interpreted by the incoming administration as a possible display of aggressive foreign adventurism.

In 1982, Reagan delivered his famous "Evil Empire" speech. A year later, in March 1983, the President announced his dream of building a huge defensive shield against ballistic missiles, a project formally titled the Strategic Defense Initiative, but nicknamed "Star Wars." Although SDI was theoretically a defense system, the Soviet Union interpreted it otherwise. Six months after the SDI announcement, the Soviets shot down Korean Air Lines Flight 007, killing 260 passengers and claiming that the

Power lines

*"We can theoretically withdraw from Lebanon; we cannot
withdraw even in theory from our reliance on the U.S. electric
power grid, the computer and telephone communications
systems, or our internal transportation networks....What is
needed now is the political awareness and will to address this
issue before a major regional or national disaster occurs.*

America's Hidden Vulnerabilities
Center for Strategic and International Studies,1984

jet was on an espionage mission in Soviet airspace. A NATO nuclear-test exercise in October (code named "Able Archer") further convinced the Soviet leaders that the United States was preparing for war. Fortunately, the situation was defused before further misinterpretations could raise the stakes.

After a lull in the late 1970s, the nation's civil defense program enjoyed a brief last hurrah under Reagan. In 1981, at the President's behest, the National Security Council developed an upgraded civil defense plan, to be implemented over seven years.[i] NSDD 23 marked the first time that an administration had set an end date for achievement of an "acceptable" level of population protection. The NSC also looked into the possibility of developing programs to protect key industries and industrial workers through provision of blast shelters—the first time that state survival, not merely population protection—had been seriously addressed. Continuity of government also received a theoretical boost: previous efforts had been restricted largely to protection of the President. Under the NSC scenario, the program was to be broadened to include more of the Federal, state, and local governmental structure—a provision that was questioned for creating a special level of protection for government leaders.

In light of Reagan's trademark hard-line stance toward the Russians, the administration's civil defense plans were viewed suspiciously in some quarters as an attempt to "make nuclear war plans credible to the Soviets and acceptable to Americans" and "to make nuclear troops out of the citizenry." The arguments echoed concerns that had been bubbling to the surface for more than forty years about civil defense being at heart more provocative than preventive. [ii] [iii]

In spite of the apparent edginess of the times, the American public was skeptical about civil defense and far less prone than it had been in the 1950s and early 1960s to respond enthusiastically to calls for reinvigorated preparedness. Two decades' worth of pop culture movies, books, and gags poking fun at the superpower stand-off had helped to inoculate many Americans against fears of nuclear annihilation. The attitude was epitomized in Director Stanley Kubrick's now-classic black comedy, Dr. Strangelove or: How I Learned to Stop Worrying and Love the Bomb (1964) and the lighter 1966 film The Russians Are Coming, The Russians are Coming. MAD magazine got into the act, too, with its long-running Spy v. Spy comic strip.

A plainspoken sentiment by Dwight Eisenhower, almost twenty years earlier, captured what many Americans surely had been feeling all along about the nation's civil defense efforts: "If I were in the finest shelter in the world, all alone, with all my family members somewhere else, I think I'd just walk out. I don't want to live in that kind of world."[iv]

Public disenchantment with Washington's handling of the Vietnam War further fueled skepticism about the wisdom of American foreign and defense policy. The Watergate (Nixon) and Contra (Reagan) scandals of the 1970s and 1980s further eroded public confidence in national leadership. When the Soviet "Evil Empire" dissolved in 1991, any lingering public and political interest in maintaining a constant state of home front war-readiness evaporated.

In the end, one of the chief legacies of the Cold War was to turn off many Americans to the entire notion of civil defense and domestic preparations for possible attacks on American soil. As the nation's principal nuclear threat (apparently) melted away with the fall of the Berlin Wall and dissolution of the U.S.S.R., plus no compelling imminent threat on the domestic front, political appetite for supporting high-profile Cold War-type civil defense programs vanished. During the strenuous budget battles in Congress in the late 1980s, fought in the context of the Graham-Rudman balanced budget amendment, civil defense lost further ground. In 1994, the 44-year old program was officially put out to pasture with the repeal of the original legislation.

"Whether it betokens healthy perspective or dangerous 'psychic numbing,' our adjustment to the half-century old specter of nuclear Armageddon has to be considered when preparing Americans for a potential terrorist attack,' wrote historian David Greenberg in Slate in February 2003. "In our post-Strangelove era, strident insistences that Americans must trust the government's invocations of national security cut no ice."[v]

**TIMELINE OF FEDERAL-LEVEL POLICYMAKING: 1980 – 1990**

**1980**—first Joint Terrorism Task Force created at FBI office in New York City. As of 2003, 66 JTTF's had been established at FBI field offices. As terrorist attacks became more difficult to assess, JTTF's were formed to facilitate cooperation and information sharing among local law enforcement and federal agents.

## A PATTERN EMERGES

The spiral downward of public interest in preparedness, however, did not mean that the world was safe. Long before the Cold War officially ended, new sources of threats abroad began to emerge—on a smaller scale than a nuclear showdown between superpowers, but frequent enough to warrant official attention and hint at a trend worth watching.

One of the highest-profile events occurred on November 4, 1979, when militant Iranian students seized the U.S. embassy in Tehran, kidnapping 66 Americans. Fifty-two of the victims were held hostage for 444 days, until their negotiated release on January 20, 1981—Reagan's inauguration day.

In January 1982, a U.S. military attache stationed at the embassy in Paris, was shot and killed by Lebanese terrorists. In August of the same year, a bomb exploded on a Pan Am jet during its approach to Honolulu Airport, killing one passenger.

In 1983, Beirut was the scene of two major terrorist attacks against U.S. targets, resulting in more than 250 American deaths. The first attack took place on April 18, 1983, when a van packed with explosives exploded in front of the U.S. Embassy, killing 63 people, including 17 Americans. Communications intercepts, combined with Lebanese interrogation of suspects, pointed a finger at Iranian and Syrian government involvement.

The second attack occurred on October 23, 1983, when the headquarters of the Marine Battalion Landing Team was destroyed by another explosives-filled truck, killing 241 people. Another bomb killed 59 at French forces headquarters nearby. Communications intercepts pointed to Iranian government involvement—specifically the Revolutionary Guards. A year later, in September 1984, a van bearing diplomatic license plates circumvented three concrete barriers in front of the U.S. Embassy annex in East Beirut and exploded. Two American military officers and twelve Lebanese were killed.

Kidnappings (and occasionally murder) of Americans in Lebanon were common in the mid-1980s. Targets included educators (such as the president of the American University in Beirut, who was killed), journalists, and ministers, plus intelligence and military officers. Airplane hijackings were also not uncommon. On June 14, 1985, TWA Flight 847 was hijacked on its way from Athens to Rome. A U.S. Navy diver on board the plane was murdered by the hijackers. The operation was directed by a member of the Iranian-backed Hezbollah ("Party of God") who also kidnapped (and later killed) CIA officer William Buckley. The high seas weren't safe either. On October 7, 1985, four Palestinian terrorists hijacked the cruise ship Achilles Lauro off of Egypt and killed a disabled American tourist, Leon Klinghoffer, throwing his body overboard together with his wheelchair. Just before Christmas, airports in Rome and Vienna were bombed, killing 20 people, five of whom were Americans. Libya was linked to the attacks.

"In the '80s, you had . . . terrorist organizations hijacking American planes and holding the planes hostages for political reasons or for release of militants or terrorists." notes Tom Falvey, who spent much of his career at the Department of Transportation in the Office of Intelligence & Security. "There were some notable killings of Americans on board these planes. . . Response [was] focused on getting the weapons out of the cabin. Then, of course, you have Pan Am 103, which put a whole different light on it."

Falvey's reference is to the bombing of Pan Am 103, also known as "Lockerbie." On December 21, 1988, the plane exploded over Lockerbie, Scotland, killing all 259 passengers and crew, and 11 residents of the village. Investigators initially suspected a number of terrorist organizations, as well as nations (including Syria and Iran), but eventually concluded that Libya masterminded the operation—most likely in retaliation for the 1986 U.S. bombing of Libya, in which Muammar Qadhafi's adopted daughter died. An explosive device encased in a tape recorder brought the Pan Am flight down.

Official response to the incident was a program to heighten the screening of checked baggage, especially on international flights. "At that point," says Falvey, "there was a lot of money being thrown to the FAA to develop explosive detection systems that would detect a very small amount of plastic explosives."

TIMELINE OF FEDERAL-LEVEL POLICYMAKING: 1980 – 1990

1982—National Security Telecommunications Advisory Committee (NSTAC) created by Executive Order 12382. The NSTAC brought together industry executives from the financial, information technology, aerospace and telecommunications industry to provide industry-based advice to the President on implementing national security and emergency preparedness in communications policy.

In spite of the drama of the Lockerbie bombing, federal response to the incident was incremental, not instantaneous or dramatic. In response to pressure from victims' families, President George H. W. Bush convened a Presidential Commission on Aviation Security and Terrorism seven months after the attack. The panel's report, issued in May 1990, cited major security flaws in the aviation security system. Nearly two years after the attack, Bush signed the Aviation Security Improvement Act.[vi]

## COMMON THREADS

What most of the hijackings and bombings of the 1980s had in common was a lack of direct relationship to the Soviet Union, specifically the Cold War stand-off between superpowers. During the long Cold War, competition between the two superpowers had helped to keep in check many low-simmering, longstanding regional instabilities. Or at least to overshadow them enough to distract attention. As the Cold War cooled off and regional problems heated up, governments and non-state players began to vie to fill the power vacuum. Nationalism, ethnicity, religion, and a host of other factors came into play in new ways. Americans traveling abroad discovered that holding a U.S. passport sometimes made them an easy, if unwitting, target of resentment against the U.S.'s reach into markets and politics around the globe.

What the increasingly violent hijackings and attacks also had in common was a reliance on tactics that fell far short of nuclear—or even conventional—military confrontation, yet were high on drama. Finding ways to strike at the powerful United States without invoking a superpower response didn't take genius, just ingenuity. All that was required was finding a suitable Achilles Heel.

Phil Lacombe, the former Staff Director of the President's Commission on Critical Infrastructure Protection, points out that nations

### TIMELINE OF FEDERAL-LEVEL POLICYMAKING: 1980 – 1990

**1985—NSDD 179** created the **Vice President's Task Force for Combating Terrorism**. The Task Force's final report in 1986 noted that important industry and government assets presented particu- larly attractive targets to terrorists. The study also acknowledged the vulnerability of the nation's technology-based infrastructure.

and other groups were learning that they could risk attacks on U.S. interests, by carefully staying under the threshold of provocation that would evoke a "Desert Storm kind of response."

"If you stay below that threshold, whatever that threshold is," explains Lacombe, "then you could put the United States in the position of not being able to assert its own will."

The build-up of a formidable military capable of sending a huge force overseas had, of course, been a calculated Cold War exercise to ensure that the United States could "assert its own will" when and where it deemed necessary or useful. During and after World War II, the federal government had intentionally nurtured a military complex of tremendous size, very much intertwined with an industrial base to support it—a "conjunction of an immense military establishment and a large arms industry...new in the American experience," noted President Dwight Eisenhower in his Farewell Address to the nation in January 1961. "The total influence—economic, political, even spiritual—is felt in every city, every statehouse, every office of the federal government."[vii]

The year after Eisenhower left office, the Cuban Missile Crisis brought the nuclear peril a bit too close for comfort, but the 1950s and 1960s otherwise generally offered little in the way of serious concern about potential attacks on U.S. soil. The civil rights, anti-Vietnam War, and environmental movements served up high-profile public protest, and sporadic violence, but dramatic developments abroad like the Korean War, Berlin Crisis and, later, Vietnam tended to reinforce the feeling that conflicts and confrontations of a truly threatening nature happened elsewhere, not inside U.S. borders.

By the early 1970s—just as many of the post-World War II mobilization programs were waning or ending—a few voices began to point out

TIMELINE OF FEDERAL-LEVEL POLICYMAKING: 1980 – 1990

1986—NSDD 207: The National Program for Combating Terrorism. This NSDD reinforced, by way of the VP Task Force for Combating Terrorism, the already established counterterrorism policy of the U.S. According to congressional testimony, NSDD 207 directed FEMA "under the auspices of the Interdepartmental Group on Terrorism, to identify the extent to which various . . . infrastructure elements (e.g. the computerized banking system, power grids, and communications networks) were vulnerable to terrorism."

that there might be more to focus on at home than just creating nuclear bomb shelters or stockpiling supplies that looked like they were never going to be used.

Although most "significant incidents" in the U.S. were attributable to "careless hunters, vandals, environmentalists, disgruntled employees, and extortionists . . . not terrorists," others were less easily dismissed or categorized. A 1989 study (hereafter referred to as the Lane report) prepared for the U.S. Senate Committee on Governmental Affairs by Secret Service employee Charles Lane, listed specific instances of pipeline bombings, transmission tower destruction and fuel tank explosions between 1969 and 1984, including several attempted bombings of the trans-Alaska pipeline between 1977 and 1980.[viii] The report postulated that "hundreds, perhaps thousands, of other minor incidents have occurred involving many of the distribution and telecommunications systems in the U.S. An accurate accounting of these incidents is difficult because there is no central repository for information, no reporting requirement, and frequently a reluctance by system owners and operators to publicize their problems."

One incident in 1969 involved a Vietnam protester who, together with three associates, dynamited four high voltage transmission lines belonging to the public service company of Colorado. The blast disrupted service to, among others, the Coors Porcelain Company plant in Golden, Colorado, which was making nose cones for U.S. missiles. The plant was on DOD's key facilities list and the man's case was tried on the basis of the Defense Production Act of 1950. He eluded capture until 1975, was tried and convicted. Upon appeal his verdict was overturned.

The year 1984 brought the first recorded bioterrorism attack on U.S. soil. The community of The Dalles (Oregon) suffered an outbreak of salmonella following the intentional contamination of local salad bars by a local religious group intent on influencing turn-out in upcoming county elections. At the time, the incident garnered little media attention because of the remoteness of the town and the involvement of a "fanatical fringe group."[ix]

## NOWHERE TO HIDE

A steady stream of government reports painted a picture of the vulnerabilities of a sprawling, open country knitted together by transportation, power and communications systems designed for efficiency not security.

A 1962 study of the electrical industry by the DEPA (Defense Electric Power Administration) suggested thorough review of all open-source material on the country's electrical grid,[x] citing the dangers of making information too readily available.

A 1970 report for DOD identified 126 'hit points' on the nation's pipeline systems which could bring the entire supply to a halt.

In 1975, the Interagency Study Group chaired by Robert H. Kupperman, a member of the Working Group of the Cabinet Committee (under Nixon), looked at the "problem of possible terrorist threats or attacks involving nuclear, chemical or biological weapons of mass destruction." The group concluded that the National Security Council needed to take the lead in addressing the issue.

Another report by the same group in January 1976 examined "intermediate terrorism"—defined as a "level of terrorist violence lying between mass destruction terrorism and . . . assassinations or abductions." Examples included use of "man-portable" missiles to destroy commercial aircraft; blowing up a nuclear power reactor; and sabotage of key elements of a multi-state electric power grid. Pointing to the upcoming Montreal Olympics, U.S. Bicentennial, and Presidential elections, the report noted that "the many public events will provide attractive targets for terrorist groups, and the movement of terrorists into and within the country will be facilitated by the heavy visitor flow. Extra vigilance should be exercised by authorities responsible for events in the form of "the judicious use of barriers, sensors, communications, and anti-terrorist materials (e.g. antitoxins)" to enhance the security of possible targets. The report also urged establishment of an "anti-terrorism management information system available to a range of federal and local law enforcement agencies" and pursuit of a number of other counterterrorism measures.[xi]

In 1978 and 1979, reports by the Congressional Research Service and General Accounting Office both described the nation's pipelines as potential targets. In 1980, FEMA contracted for a study titled "State of the Art Report on Vulnerability to Terrorism of U.S. Resource Systems." The Department of Energy in 1981 received a report underscoring that the nation's power systems were vulnerable to "malevolent attack." Similar reports in 1982 by the GAO focused on the electric power grid.

A 1981 book, Brittle Power: Energy Strategy for National Security, provided an "alarming analysis of the terrorist threat to power lines, power stations and substations," noted a 1984 paper on the electrical grid and defense needs. "Not only are they vulnerable to destruction if an incentive exists, but with the resources available to terrorists today, from automatic weapons to hand held bazookas and shoulder-fired precision guided missiles, it would make defense of current facilities next to impossible." [xii]

Perhaps the most compelling report was a no-nonsense study in 1984 by the Center for Strategic and International Studies (CSIS) at Georgetown University titled "America's Hidden Vulnerabilities: Crisis Management in a Society of Networks." The study's chairman was R. James Woolsey; co-chair was the same Robert H. Kupperman (regarded by some as the "father of counterrorism") who had headed the 1975 Interagency Study Group of the Cabinet Committee. Al Gore, Jr., then a House member, served on the CSIS Science and Technology Committee which produced the report. The report, which laid out in unsentimental language the dangers of terrorism to the nation's networks, was written not long after the bombings of U.S. sites in Beirut in 1983. [xiii]

"We can theoretically withdraw from Lebanon," warned the CSIS report, "[W]e cannot withdraw even in theory from our reliance on the U.S. electric power grid, the computer and telephone communications systems, or our internal transportation networks. . . .What is needed now is the political awareness and will to address this issue before a major regional or national disaster occurs. [xiv]

## COMING TO GRIPS

The level of "political awareness and will" on the scale urged by the CSIS report was not immediately forthcoming. But the Reagan administration was taking what it felt were important steps to address the growing potential for terrorism.

One immediate effort involved dealing with the fall-out of the creation of FEMA in 1979. Signed while Carter was still in office, Executive

**TIMELINE OF FEDERAL-LEVEL POLICYMAKING: 1980 – 1990**

1987—Computer Security Act assigned the National Institute for Standards and Technology responsibility for developing security standards and guidelines for sensitive information in government computers.

1987—DARPA, under Department of Defense, created the Computer Emergency Response Team (CERT) at Carnegie Mellon University.

Order 12148 assigned FEMA the responsibility to supervise and pull together under one administrative roof all of the federal government's disparate and disjointed programs and measures for dealing with a wide range of emergencies, as well as the physical security of key facilities.

The theory, perhaps, was correct; but the request proved to be overwhelming. The agency—barely pulled together itself—not only had its own administrative nightmare to deal with, but met with resistance when it tried to become "become the single most important organization in the federal government's structure to deal with NSEP (National Security

## When Disaster Strikes: A Brief History of FEMA[1]

'*D*isaster management' has meant different things at different times in the United States. From responding to natural disasters to promoting civil defense duck-and-cover campaigns, responsibility for preparing for or picking up the pieces when disaster strikes has bounced from agency to agency, usually at the whim of the White House.[2]

■ *Congressional Act of 1803 – first piece of disaster legislation to make federal money available to state and local communities.[3] The legislation was used on an ad hoc basis for a century to respond to natural disasters.[4]*

■ *1949 Federal Civil Defense Administration—established initially in the Executive Office of the President (EOP) for the purpose of monitoring disasters and emergencies. Its responsibilities focused on civil defense and domestic emergency management, but offered no direct assistance to states and local governments.[5]*

■ *1950 Federal Disaster Relief Act—passed by Congress to authorize the use of federal resources to state and local communities after their own resources had been exhausted and a governor had requested assistance from the President.*

■ *1950 Office of Defense Mobilization—assumed responsibilities for defense production activities and emergency relief. The earlier FCDA retained responsibility for preparing the civilian population for nuclear attack.[6]*

■ *1950 – 1961—several reorganizations of emergency preparedness and civil defense programs—responsibilities bounced back and forth among different agencies and in and out of the White House.[7]*

Emergency Planning) and other emergencies of a national scope."[xv] Established departments, particularly Justice, Defense and Treasury, fought the new agency's efforts. Many saw FEMA as just another layer of bureaucracy. In no time the agency found itself paralyzed by politics both internal and external.[xvi]

While the difficulties at FEMA heated up, the bombings in Beirut prompted formation of a Vice Presidential Task Force on Combating Terrorism, launched by NSDD 179 in July 1985. The interagency task force, headed by then-Vice President George Bush, was composed of the

■ 1960s – 1970s—series of amendments to Federal Disaster Relief Act passed in response to several large-scale natural disasters. The amendments were also part of an ongoing effort to define federal emergency response activities.

■ 1979 Creation of FEMA—pushed by the National Governors Association and authorized by President Jimmy Carter. Consolidated more than one hundred offices and programs throughout the federal government with responsibility for disaster relief.

■ 1979 – 2001—FEMA wrestled with internal disagreements, interagency politics and a series of disasters, prompting the agency's leadership to rethink its emergency management approach, particularly its role in national security strategy.

■ March 2003—FEMA was absorbed by the new Department of Homeland Security, formed in November 2002.

[1] For details of federal, state and local disaster policy making, see www.disaster-timeline.com
[2] Sylves, Richard and William Cumming, "FEMA's Path to Homeland Security: 1979 – 2003," Journal of Homeland Security, 2004, Vol. 1, Issue 2
[3] "Disaster Management in the 21st Century", GWU Institute for Crisis, Disaster and Risk Management, Disaster Newsletter Website, Volume 1, No. 3 at: http://www.seas.gwu.edu/~emse232/emse232book3
[4] "FEMA History," Federal Emergency Management Agency at: http://www.fema.gov/about/history.shtm
[5] "The History of Civil Defense & Emergency Management in Tennessee," Tennessee Emergency Management Agency at: www.tnema.org/archives/emHistory/TNCD History3.htm
[6] Ibid.
[7] See "The History of Civil Defense & Emergency Management in Tennessee" for more detail about this period.

Secretaries of State, Treasury, Defense and Transportation; the Attorney General; the Director of the FBI; the Director of Central Intelligence; the Director of OMB; Assistant to the President for National Security Affairs; the Chairman of the Joint Chiefs of Staff; the Chief of Staff to the VP; the Assistant to the VP for National Security Affairs; the Executive Director of the Task Force; and "others as appropriate."

In 1986, the Vice President's Task Force issued its classified final report, apparently echoing many of the same concerns raised by the CSIS report two years earlier. Phil Lacombe and David Keyes, writing in The Journal of Homeland Security in October 2000, credit the task force with appreciating that "key industry and government assets presented attractive targets to terrorists. The report also grasped how vulnerability resulted from openness inherent in our society and its highly sophisticated infra-structure: the intricate, interrelated networks supporting transportation, energy, communications, finance, industry, medicine, defense, diploma-cy, and government."[xvii]

While the Task Force toiled away, the National Security Council took charge of the fractious FEMA situation. In September 1985, it created a Senior Interagency Group on National Security Emergency Preparedness (SIG-NSEP) to replace a cumbersome Emergency Mobilization Preparedness Board thathad been created in 1981 and dragged into the FEMA power struggle. The SIG-NSEP included representatives from Justice, Defense, Treasury and OMB, and was headed by the Assistant to the President for National Security Affairs.

Four months later, in January 1986, the National Security Council issued NSDD 207 (National Program for Combating Terrorism). The NSDD, among many other things, directed FEMA, under the auspices of the Interdepartmental Group on Terrorism, to identify the extent to which

TIMELINE OF FEDERAL-LEVEL POLICYMAKING: 1980 – 1990

1988—Executive Order 12656 signed by President Reagan creating a new Federal Emergency Plan. The EO assigned emergency response responsibilities to various federal agencies.
1988—Robert T. Stafford Disaster Relief and Emergency Assistance Act (known as the 'Stafford Act') enhanced the Disaster Relief Act of 1974 by incorporating non-natural disasters (to a limited degree) into the list of emergencies for which the fed-eral government will cost-share with State and local governments.

various infrastructure elements were vulnerable to terrorism and "propose near and long term solutions." As a follow-up, in April 1986, SIG-NSEP created interagency groups to focus on policy issues in 1) civil defense, 2) national mobilization, and 3) energy vulnerability. The Committee of Principals of the 33-year old National Communications System was designated the fourth interagency group, and was to focus on telecommunications. In response to requests from the National Security Council, FEMA apparently submitted two requested reports on near and long term plans for infrastructure protection, including one in April 1987 that proposed a National Asset Protection Plan, suggesting an initial FY88 funding of $2 million and 7 employees.[xviii]

By then, however, FEMA had lost its ambitious battle to become the lead agency in the nation's counterterrorism efforts. In September 1987, the National Security Council issued a memorandum setting NSEP priorities for January 1987 through January 1989, one of which was reassignment of protection responsibilities for key assets from FEMA back to individual federal departments and agencies. Another was to establish government-industry plans to minimize the impact of energy disruptions. The arrangement was finalized on November 18, 1988 when Reagan signed EO 12656, creating a new Federal Emergency Plan ("Assignment of Emergency Preparedness Responsibilities") and detailing the responsibilities of various departments in the executive branch.[xix]

Under the new plan, the National Security Council was in charge of overall strategy and the Director of FEMA was to assist by implementing national security emergency preparedness policy. The Department of Justice effectively took over the earlier role that FEMA had not been able to handle. The plan's Sec. 1102. Support Responsibilities stipulated that the "Attorney General of the United States shall: (1) Assist the heads of Federal departments and agencies, State and local governments, and the private sector in the development of plans to physically protect essential resources and facilities." The Executive Order defined a "national security emergency" as any occurrence that "seriously degrades or threatens the national security of the United States."[xx]

FEMA's ill-fated bid to become the lead agency in dealing with terrorism had probably been decided as early as 1982, when NSDD 30 designated the Federal Bureau of Investigation as the "lead agency for counterterrorism in the United States." (The thrust of PDD 30, however, was aimed at incidents overseas.) In 1983 the FBI was given new jurisdiction involving the construction of energy facilities. The Comprehensive Crime Control Act (1984) and the Diplomatic Security and Anti-Terrorism Act (1986) gave even more territory to the FBI. In 1989, the Lane report characterized the FBI as having "more jurisdiction than ever in history to deal with terrorist groups or members."[xxi]

In 1988, an FBI official testified before the Senate Judiciary Subcommittee on Technology and the Law, noting that the FBI was developing initiatives to better address the problems of potential terrorist attacks against any element of the infrastructure. One initiative involved an attempt to develop a domestic terrorist threat warning system. An office at the Department of Energy—the Office of Threat Assessments—had tried disseminating advisories through organizations representing the common interest of the industry, such as the North American Electric Reliability Council (NERC).[xxii] But after at least one incident in which a miscommunication resulted in an overreaction, the FBI took over the responsibility of reviewing State Department messages and determining whether an advisory should be sent to industry.[xxiii]

Another Department of Justice effort involved a program called the Key Assets Initiative (KAI). The objective of KAI was to develop a database of information on "key assets" within the jurisdiction of each FBI field office, establish lines of communications with asset owners and operators to improve both cyber and physical protection, and to coordinate with relevant authorities to ensure their participation.

The KAI program was far from novel. DOD and the Department of Commerce were among those who had been at pains since at least the early 1950s to try to create lists of facilities vital to defense and national security. Commerce had compiled a Critical Industrial Facilities list as part of its IEB ratings program in the early 1950s. DOD had its own Key Facilities List composed of critical defense related industrial and manu-facturing facilities in the private sector. "Facilities placed on this list were sponsored by a component of the armed forces," explained the Lane report, "and the owner/operator voluntarily accepted the designation and associated responsibilities, including a requirement to allow the Defense Investigative Service to conduct on-site physical security surveys." [xxiv]

In the early 1980s, during the period of high tension with the U.S.S.R., DOD had expanded the program beyond essential facilities to include the "supporting energy base" for the operation of industrial sites important to DOD. The move was a fresh acknowledgment that key industrial facilities alone weren't the only thing worth protecting—without electricity, gas or other energy supplies, the facilities would be forced to shut down.[xxv] Defense Energy Memorandum 83-1 established energy supply assurance as its highest priority for the first time.

In 1989, the DOD program was renamed the Key Assets Protection Program (KAPP) and a classified Key Assets List was developed. The list identified "those facilities which will be protected under a program requiring national guard or state reserve units, acting under the direction of a state area command (STARC), to protect designated facilities while mobilizing for future commitment."[xxvi]

The KAPP program, and related Key Assets List, had its share of skeptics. Critics pointed out that even under a mobilization scenario, there was reason to doubt that National Guard or reserve units would have sufficient manpower to guard the designated facilities. The reasoning wasn't without precedent: In both World Wars the military had been flooded with requests from the private sector clamoring for special protection. The KAL was also incomplete: A number of facilities under the control of one of DOD's own agencies—the Corps of Engineers—didn't appear on any list because they were neither strictly military nor strictly civilian.

The very existence of lists of critical assets was also—as always—a subject of debate. Agencies and departments often had different philosophies and sensibilities, at different times, about the value and wisdom of list-making.

DOD tried to deal with the problem of creating a dangerous "master target list" by dividing its Key Assets List by military districts, with limited distribution. Other agencies eschewed compiling lists entirely. FEMA and DOE allegedly did not feel the need "to establish a national list of critical nodes which would be held by one or more federal agencies. Both are

**TIMELINE OF FEDERAL-LEVEL POLICYMAKING: 1980 – 1990**

**1988**—'High-Tech Terrorism' hearings held by the Senate Judiciary Subcommittee on Technology and Law.
**1989**—'The Vulnerability of Telecommunications and Energy Resources to Terrorism," prepared by special staff investigator Charles C. Lane and presented to the Senate Committee on Governmental Affairs in February, warned of widespread security weaknesses in two key sectors of the nation's infrastructure.

content to initiate activities which cause the utilities to identify and take actions to mitigate their own vulnerabilities," said the Lane report."[xxvii]

The Department of Transportation was also set against the idea, at least in the 1990s, according to Tom Falvey:

> "We in DOT strongly objected to [the] development of lists.... If you take critical nodes, critical facilities, most of which are owned by the private sector...there's some assumption that you're going to do something with that. The Key Asset Protection Program [at DOD] had a list about 1,100 assets.... Are you going to put National Guard troops [around every facility] when there's a certain threat? And what level threat?... So you've got to have a national policy.... Otherwise, the list becomes a source of compromise. What if that list wound up in The Washington Post or wound up in the hands of a terrorist and that information became public knowledge, so now you have a complete target set. I mean, what a perfect thing for a foreign intelligence organization to want to target is this list. Can you really protect it? And the way stuff works in Washington, it didn't seem that it was a very good idea."

To some degree, the creation of lists—as always, at least before the terrorist attacks on September 11, 2001—was an exercise in closing the barn door after the cow had made its merry escape: An incredible amount of information was available from public sources, a feature of the nation's open society.

Although the Defense Electric Power Administration had urged as early as 1962 that information about power systems be made difficult to obtain, detailed maps of the electrical power grids could be retrieved from the Superintendent of Documents as late as 1978. And even later from

**TIMELINE OF FEDERAL-LEVEL POLICYMAKING:** 1980 – 1990

**1989**—Presidential Commission on Aviation Security and Terrorism created in response to Pan Am #103. The Commission recommended a significant upgrade in airline security, plus a "zero tolerance" policy towards terrorists, including preemptive strikes on terrorist enclaves in harboring nations.

**1990**—Aviation Security Improvement Act codified the recommendations of the Presidential Commission on Aviation Security and Terrorism.

other sources. Up to the late 1980s, the Strategic Petroleum Reserve was publishing quarterly and annual reports indicating specific draw-down capabilities by facility and mode.

Mock terrorist exercises also often provided eye-openers. For example, in 1987, U.S. Army Special Forces team was able to knock out several power substations using nothing more than publicly-available information to plan the attack. The eleven "terrorists" suffered no casualties while the defenders recorded fifty-three.[xxviii] The team had gotten much of its information from a university library.[xxix]

## THE PERENNIAL ISSUE:
## PRIVATE OWNERSHIP VS. PUBLIC INTEREST

The freely-available information pointed up another fact of life about the nation's major networks: they were—and are—by and large owned and operated by the private sector.

The Lane report put it bluntly: "The basic fact to be recognized is that the development of these networks was not a response to a national security need, but rather an economic venture designed to generate profit. Private industry does not plan, build, or protect its facilities with national security considerations in mind."[xxx] Exceptions, of course, were defense-intensive businesses that needed to meet DOD security requirements to remain in the procurement loop. Such strictures were not mandatory for businesses such as utilities whose customer base was broader.

The report went on: "Many industry officials are not overly concerned with the possibility of terrorist instigated disruptions. They argue that it is in their own interest to provide a reliable service, and that adequate redundancy and planning have been built into the systems to allow for reasonable levels of disruption."

The government had also not presented a compelling case: "[M]any officials within industry are not convinced that a serious threat really exists.... [T]here is little dissemination of information within the private sector regarding assaults…which would help create a general awareness within industry. Even when the potential threat is acknowledged, industry officials believe that if there are expenses to be incurred simply to ensure survivability of the networks in a hostile environment, those costs should be the responsibility of the federal government."

Industry had also concluded, based on its own experience, that "physically protecting a network against any and all possible disruptions is economically impossible." Emphasis was placed on restoration, not prevention.

"Industry and government officials may not even agree on the importance of a particular mode or facility," the report pointed out. "An industry representative may consider a node critical because of its importance to the operation of the total system; a defense official may consider another node more critical because it supports a vital defense related activity."

DOD was well aware that utilities such as electric and gas didn't always share its priorities or agree with its efforts. In 1975, Colonial Pipeline withdrew from the Key Facilities List—the only major pipeline in the program. That same year, a few electric utilities began to add key substations and generating stations to the DOD list (a total of 2,000), but removed them in 1980. One of the reasons cited for withdrawal was the perception that DOD personnel weren't qualified to conduct physical security surveys on electrical facilities. Another reason suggested was that the utilities felt that they "got little out of the program while being required to conform to federal requirements."[xxxi] Another reason given was that being included in the KFL gave them a false sense of security by implying that the federal government would supply protection—not something the government could or would agree to.

After losing the pipeline and the electrical owners, DOD attempted to woo them back with a program that didn't require on-site inspections. Instead, critical nodes in the energy industry were identified by DOD and then pointed out to system owners—similar to a program that the Business and Defense Services Administration had touted in the 1950s. The tweaked program also educated state area commanders about the nodes so that plans could be developed to protect them, with or without owner cooperation. The prospect of actually having to act to protect the nodes flew in the face of DOD's long and concerted campaign to avoid becoming enmeshed in private sector security during wartime. But if push came to shove, DOD wanted to be ready.

Elbow grease notwithstanding—good intentions, too—the DOD program nonetheless suffered from a syndrome that plagues every governmental effort to be comprehensive and current—including BDSA's energetic efforts thirty years earlier: Thanks to constant turnover in the defense industry, a list made yesterday, distributed today, was guaranteed to be out of date tomorrow.

<sup>i</sup> National Security Decision Directive (NSDD) 23 essentially endorsed Presidential Decision Directive (PDD) 41, signed earlier by President Jimmy Carter. In keeping with traditional Congressional ambivalence about civil defense, Carter's proposed budget for the civil defense program was not supported. Reagan's program fared no better. By 1983, the Reagan administration shifted its focus to development of the Integrated Emergency Management System, an all-hazards approach that stressed preparations for a full spectrum of emergencies, from hurricanes to nuclear power plant accidents. See Wayne B. Blanchard, American Civil Defense 1945-1884: The Evolution of Programs and Policies (Emmitsburg, Maryland: National Emergency Center, Monograph Series, Volume 2 Number 2, 1985) 20-24.

<sup>ii</sup> Blanchard (1985) 22.

<sup>iii</sup> NSDD 23 also marked the first time that the use of civil defense funds for peacetime disaster was authorized.

<sup>iv</sup> Congressional Record, 17 September 1963.

<sup>v</sup> David Greenberg, "Fallout Can Be Fun: How the Cold War Civil-Defense Programs Became Farce," Slate (20 February 2003) <http://slate.msn.com/id/2078892>.

<sup>vi</sup> In August 1989, President George H.W. Bush issued Executive Order 12686, forming the seven-member Presidential Commission on Aviation Security and Terrorism, in response to the downing of Pan Am 103 in December 1988. Conclusions of the Commission in its 182-page report included a "zero tolerance" policy, including preparation for "preemptive retaliatory military strikes against terrorist enclaves in nations that harbor them." The report also recommended a top-to-bottom revamping of the U.S. government's airline security apparatus and creation of a new assistant secretary of transportation for security and intelligence, plus a federal security manager post at each major airport. Falvey's employer, the Office of Intelligence & Security at Department of Transportation, was part of the new apparatus.

<sup>vii</sup> Eisenhower's precedessor, Harry Truman, had helped to set the "conjunction"'in motion with such measures as the Defense Production Act of 1950 and 1952's Executive Order 10421, which required federal agencies to "develop and execute programs and measures for the physical security of designated facilities important to national mobilization," under the auspices of the National Security Resources Board.

<sup>viii</sup> Charles Lane, untitled draft, Committee Report, United States Senate, Committee on Governmental Affairs (9 February 1989).

<sup>ix</sup> Claire B. Rubin, William R. Cumming, Irmak Renda-Tanali, and Thomas Birkland, Major Terrorism Events and Their Outcomes (1988-2001) (Arlington, Virginia: June 2003) 16. See also <www.disaster-timeline.com>.

<sup>x</sup> Arkady Shevchenko, the former Soviet Undersecretary General for Political and security Council Affairs, at UN, until he defected once said that the the U.S.S.R., in addition to KGB and GRU agents as part of the UN staff, also "harbors agents of a group called VS. These agents specialize in studying utilities, bridges and other critical facilities as sabotage candidates in the event of war. Shevchenko stated that after the NY blackout (1965), a couple of agents from VS were drunk and told him that "We can black out the whole east coast." (Michael A. Aimone and Thomas P. Myers, Can We Work in the Dark?: The Impact of Constrained Electric Service on Critical Defense Industries (Washington: Industrial College of the Armed Forces, May 1984) 34.)

<sup>xi</sup> Robert A. Fearey to Thomas Eagleburger, briefing memorandum, "Intermediate Terrorism," draft, undated (1975?). Photocopy from Collections of the Gerald R. Ford Library.

xii Aimone and Myers 33.

xiii Robert Kupperman also gave a speech in 1983 to the Edison Electric Institute, issuing a warning about potential retaliation for U.S. policy in Lebanon.

xiv James R. Woolsey and Robert H. Kupperman, America's Hidden Vulnerabilities: Crisis Management in a Society of Networks (Washington: Center for Strategic and International Studies, Georgetown University, October 1984).

xv Lane 86.

xvi FEMA did get far enough by 1984 to have developed the concept for a National Facilities Security Program, the basis of which would have been the Department of Defense's Key Assets List. (Aimone and Myers 65.)

xvii Phil Lacombe and David Keyes, "Defending the American Homeland's Infrastructure," Journal of Homeland Security (October 2000). <http://www.homeland-security.org/journal/articles/lacombe.htm>.

xviii Lane 89.

xix Executive Order 12656 revoked Executive Order 10421, the 1952 order that had stipulated that all agencies establish plans for protecting assets in their jurisdictions that were important to war mobilization. It also revoked Executive Order 11490 from 1969, a later version of Executive Order 10421.

xx Because of its relationship to the nuclear power industry, the Department of Energy (DOE) was specifically tasked in Executive Order 12656 with identifying "energy facilities essential to the mobilization, deployment and sustainment of resources to support the national security and national welfare, and develop energy supply and demand strategies to ensure continued provision of minimum essential services in national security emergencies."

xxi Lane 99.

xxii NERC was formed in 1968 as part of the electrical industry's response to the embarrassing 1965 black-out.

xxiii Lane 96.

xxiv Lane 90.

xxv From a student's paper for the Industrial College of the Armed Forces in 1956: "It is almost pertinent to recognize that though a given plant or other facility may survive but is without utilities or operators, it is useless unless these elements are again made available.... It is essential to plan for all elements—plant utilities, materials and personnel.... Less that this is sheer gambling on bombing odds." [Frank Collins, Jr., National Survival Through Dispersal (Washington: Industrial College of the Armed Forces, 26 March 1956, Term Paper No. 303): 15.

xxvi Lane 89.

xxvii Lane 40.

xxviii Lane 43.

xxix While researching his dissertation at George Mason University in the late 1990s, Ph.D. candidate Sean Gorman put together a fairly detailed map of the country's information infrastructure, using only public sources. His success in charting vulnerabilities demonstrated how much potentially sensitive material was freely available to anyone willing to do a little research. In an article on July 8, 2003, the Washington Post dubbed Gorman's dissertation a "terrorist's treasure map." ABC interviewed Gorman on February 14, 2004: <http://www.abc.net.au/rn/science/buzz/stories/s1047647.htm>.

xxx Lane 70.

xxxi Lane 90.

# CHAPTER 5

# Wake-up Call:

## The Emergence of High-Tech Terrorism

*"The United States is a society totally dependent on interlocking networks and nodes for communications, transportation, energy transmission, financial transactions, and essential government and public services. Disruption of key nodes by terrorists could cause havoc, untold expense, and perhaps even mass deaths. We are, in the jargon of the trade, a 'target-rich environment.'"*

Senator Patrick Leahy (1990)

f rapid turnover in the address book of the defense industry was hard to keep up with in the 1980s, it paled in comparison to the accelerating pace of technological change everywhere. Computers, which had emerged during World War II for defense-related applications (cumbersome, slow and expensive), had evolved by the 1970s into standard equipment in most businesses for a wide variety of applications.

The growing presence of computer technology was helped along by the launch in the 1960s of SCADA (Supervisory Control and Data Acquisition) and process control systems for industry and utilities. The Internet got its start, too, in the 1960s when DOD commissioned its fledgling Advanced Research Projects Agency (ARPA) to begin development of a network to link research sites around the world. Software and hardware start-ups proliferated, some of which were destined to become everyday brands and household names.

Development of the single-chip microprocessor in the 1970s drove down costs to a point at which personal computers boomed alongside business units. As the size and pricetag of computers shrank, usage, applications and related software mushroomed. In 1982 *Time* magazine named the personal computer its "Man of the Year." A year later, an estimated 10 million computers were in use in the United States. By 1990 that number had climbed to 54 million, the same year that Microsoft became the first company to exceed $1 billion in sales. In 1995, when the company released its Windows 95 software, the program sold more than a million copies in its first four days.

The proliferation of computers opened a new era in the ways humans could connect with each other and control their environment, while speeding up communication, enhancing efficiency, and spawning communities.

But, as with many improvements, computers came with a downside—in forms not readily apparent, but which would soon make themselves felt.

"The pace of change, the pace of deployment of information technology [was] such that we could not keep up with it," explains Phil Lacombe. "And it all happened without our being aware of what was happening. It doesn't mean there weren't really smart people in academia and elsewhere who were thinking about it, who saw it, who understood it and who tried to raise red flags.... That was certainly the case, but as a nation, as a government, we didn't understand it. We didn't realize that as you pursue the tremendous economic benefits of information systems, you are creating vulnerabilities and dependencies that carried their own seeds of destruction."

Among the problems that followed in the wake of the computer juggernaut were spamming, fraud, deliberate circumvention of computer

TIMELINE OF FEDERAL-LEVEL POLICYMAKING: 1991 – 1995

1991—Defense Directive 3600.1 launched a formal defensive information warfare program.
1991—Nations Security Information Exchange (NSIE) created as a subcommittee to the NSTAC. The role of the NSIE is to bring government and industry leaders together to discuss vulnerabilities and electronic intrusions in a confidential forum.
1994—PDD 29 created the Security Policy Board to examine current national security structure and evaluate new and existing threats and vulnerabilities.

security systems, authorized access, industrial espionage, plus thefts of identify, money and data.

And, of course, headline-grabbing worms and viruses.

"[F]ailures or problems that begin at a modest scale can propagate along and across interlocking networks with exponential effects," warned Robert Kupperman in 1984 in a CSIS essay titled "Technological Advances and Consequent Dangers: Growing Threats to Civilization."[i] Although Kupperman wasn't referring to worms and viruses—which had yet to become a problem—his comment proved prescient.

Those most deeply involved in computer applications touching on national security were naturally more sensitized to the problems that might come with storing and sending data using systems not entirely under government control. To address such concerns, DOD's National Security Agency (NSA) founded its Department of Defense Computer Security Center in 1981. Now called the National Computer Security Center, NCSC evaluated computing equipment for high security application to ensure that facilities processing classified or other material employed trusted computer systems and components. In 1983, the NCSC issued the first DOD "Trusted Computer System Evaluation Criteria" manual, commonly referred to as the Orange Book. David Jones, who worked at NSA for much of his career, notes that the NCSC was a "big jump, big shot in the arm to computer security at the national level" when it debuted.

A few years later, in 1987, the first attempt at broad federal-level legislation to deal with issues related to security of the government's own computers was passed—the Computer Security Act of 1987. The act assigned the Commerce Dept, via the National Institute of Standards and Technology (NIST), responsibility for developing security standards and guidelines for sensitive information in government computers. One notable exemption were the national security-related networks of the Department of Defense, which felt strongly about maintaining its own security standards and already had the NCSC.

Congress had earlier passed a law to deal with computer fraud and "abuse." Stevan Mitchell, who was with DOJ at the time, notes that "the federal government was really just looking to do a stopgap measure. They understood that the states already had their own state computer crime laws on the books…but they wanted to have federal penalties and enhanced penalties for crimes that specifically involved federal interest computers, including . . . government computers, military computers, computers used in the banking and regulated industries. . . .That served the government's interest well, I think, through the late '80s and early '90s."

As the 1990s unfolded, more challenges evolved in the arena of trying to track down sophisticated computer intrusions that jumped across jurisdictional lines or used very subtle methods to evade detection. The 1984 computer fraud and abuse statute was amended in 1994 and 1996 to keep up with the advances by which "people could reach out and touch other computers throughout the nation and internationally," notes Mitchell.

As computers proliferated, along with networks, across the public and private sector, authorities were hard-pressed on many fronts to deal with attendant problems of intrusions, thefts, and manipulation of data. Even with laws on the books to deal with certain problems, there was often no recognition or no acknowledgment that a problem existed. This was especially true in the private sector, which could cite many reasons for not airing intrusions into its computer systems. Many of them were the same reasons given for not reporting physical break-ins: embarrassment, fear of lowered public confidence, an assumption that such intrusions would be rare and controllable, or that attention (and dollars) should be earmarked for restoration, not trying to prevent something that might not happen.

In late 1988, two things happened that grabbed public attention, at least for the moment. One was the Pan Am 103 (Lockerbie) bombing in December. The other, a month earlier, arrived in the wily form of the Morris worm, launched by a graduate student at Cornell University and released on November 2, 1988. The worm quickly infected 6,000 computers across the U.S. It shook up DOD sufficiently to help hurry along the creation of the Computer Emergency Response Team (CERT) at Carnegie-Mellon. CERT's birth seemed to be timely: In 1988 only 6 incidents were reported; in 1995, there were 2,412.

Just two months before the Morris worm insinuated its way into history, the Senate Judiciary Committee's Subcommittee on Technology and the Law convened hearings titled "High-Tech Terrorism." The hearings focused primarily on physical threats, and had included questions about a hypothetical scenario eerily similar to the Lockerbie bombing three months later. Says David Keyes, formerly with the FBI and now with the private sector: "Those hearings were intended to be primarily focused on physical infrastructures, bombing pipelines, blowing up bridges, sort of the old OSS mentality of behind the lines covert groups or guerrillas . . . Russian special forces that would disrupt critical communication transportation and other infrastructure nodes during transition to war, or war."

The hearings also included just enough discussion of information technologies to plant a seed. "One of the unexpected outcomes," says Keyes, "was a beginning realization of the threat represented by information technologies and the extent to which information technologies might be an easier target to damage than the physical infrastructures they controlled. Nonetheless, I would say that the output of the hearings was 98 percent physical terrorism risks and a 2 percent dawning awareness that there might be difficulty in other areas."

In 2000, Senator Patrick Leahy reflected back on the 1988 "High-Tech Terrorism" hearings and credited them with raising his awareness that "merely 'hardening' our physical space from potential attack would only prompt committed criminals and terrorists to switch tactics and use new technologies to reach vulnerable softer targets, such as our computer system and other critical infrastructures."[ii]

In an earlier statement made just a year and half after the "High-Tech Terrorism" hearings, he chided his colleagues for the lack of serious follow-up, "despite a lot of talk and a lot of planning."

"We still have not got ourselves truly ready for what is likely to be a major long term threat to the security of the United States," said Leahy. "We offer an inviting, highly vulnerable target to the sophisticated international terrorist. The United States is a society totally dependent on interlocking networks and nodes for communications, transportation, energy transmission, financial transactions, and essential government and public services. Disruption of key nodes by terrorists could cause havoc, untold expense, and perhaps even mass deaths. We are, in the jargon of the trade, a 'target-rich environment.'"

TIMELINE OF FEDERAL-LEVEL POLICYMAKING: 1991 – 1995

1994—Defense Science Board released "Information Architecture for the Battlefield" indicating that the cyber threat goes beyond criminal and hacking activity.

1994—Executive Order 12919: National Defense Industrial Resources Preparedness renewed the Defense Production Act of 1950 after its lapse during the Persian Gulf War (1990-91).

At the time of Leahy's 1990 comments, the nation was about to go to war in the Persian Gulf in two back-to-back operations: Operations Desert Shield and Desert Storm. The display of U.S. military might was impressive: 700,000 soldiers and a mind-boggling amount of equipment were shipped to the Middle East to force Iraq to back-down from its recent invasion of Kuwait.

Among other things, the two military operations staged by DOD were made-for-television examples of high-tech war on the modern battlefield. The Global Positioning System aided coalition units trekking across the desert. Advances in bombing navigation ("smart bombs") were credited by the Department of Defense with limiting civilian casualties. Audiences around the world watched some of the gadgetry at work from the safety and comfort of their own homes. The show no doubt far exceeded the expectations of at least one colonel who, in 1957 in a term paper for the Industrial College of the Armed Forces, had predicted:

The teaming of many electronic data processing systems (EDPS) throughout a web of modern high-speed communications, and integral with many modern equipments, is the magic black box that will enable the commander to regain command of the battlefield, of rear areas, and of the zone of the interior.[iii]

Efficient methods for crippling the enemy's infrastructure—power and water, for example—were also part of the operations. DOD had been working for years on "smarter ways to target," says Brent Greene, who was with DOD at the time. "We were looking at ways that you could integrate various things, as well as techniques where you could attack a particular infrastructure without ever touching the infrastructure you're really attacking. For example, if you took down a control system, you might be able to take down the thing that it controlled without ever touching the thing that it controlled. Those kinds of things are what we were looking at and so we were trying to advance a bunch of those things offensively . . . We were exploiting vulnerabilities that were based on technology."

In the process, says Greene, it was inevitable that "we started looking at it in the context that the more technologically advanced a nation is, the greater its potential vulnerability. We started saying 'We need to look at the vulnerability of the U.S.' We started completely changing around our approach, [which] had been using highly classified technologies. [Instead,] we said, 'Let's look at: If I were a bad guy, what kind of information might I be able to gain access to? What is the open source information that I could utilize to identify the vulnerability of a particular infrastructure?'"

The evolution in Greene's thinking led him and two colleagues to push for an office devoted to infrastructure protection inside DOD. "It was a one-person shop initially," notes Greene, who ran it. "The office was called the Infrastructure Protection Directorate. Critical infrastructure was a term that probably emerged in early 1995, mid-1995. I can't remember who coined it."

The term critical infrastructure, in fact, seems to have made its first appearance in Charles Lane's 1989 report to the Senate's Committee on Governmental Affairs—the report that raised many of the infrastructure issues that Greene's tiny Infrastructure Protection Directorate wanted to explore.[iv]

Greene's office began to run hypothetical scenarios similar to the eye-opening Special Forces exercise in 1987 which had depended on nothing but publicly-available information to launch a successful assault on part of the electrical power grid.

"We looked at scenarios of how to dump electric power to Wall Street, how to dump electric power to Washington, how to dump telecom in New York City, how to dump telecom in Washington," says Greene. "We started doing open source data to identify how stuff could be targeted."

While Greene and his colleagues ran their scenarios and began to quietly brief anyone who would listen, disaster struck: a Ryder rental truck packed with explosives detonated on the second level of the basement parking garage under the World Trade Center on February 26, 1993.

Although not apparently aimed at infrastructure, per se, the bombing was intended both to wreak damage and send a message. The mastermind of the plot, Ramzi Yousef, had hoped to collapse one tower into another, but fell short of his objective. Nonetheless, six people were killed and more than 1,000 were injured. Suddenly, the nation's vulnerability to domestic terrorism literally hit home.

Two years later, a similar, but deadlier assault in the American heartland catapulted terrorism into the headlines again. This time the target was federal property—the Alfred P. Murrah Federal Building in downtown Oklahoma City. Local responders, fire fighters, police force, Urban Search and Rescue Teams rushed to scene; within seven hours, President Bill Clinton ordered deployment of local, state, and federal resources. Clinton also invoked presidential authority under the Stafford Act—the first such use—assigning FEMA primary federal responsibility for responding to a domestic consequence management incident. On April 26, 1995, Clinton declared the bombing a major disaster.[v]

Brent Greene recalls the moment of the Oklahoma City bombing very well: He and a colleague were giving a critical infrastructure briefing to a Coast Guard admiral. "We interrupted the briefing to turn on CNN to see what happened. Just a curious example that when the Murrah bombing happened, we were briefing critical infrastructure stuff to the guy in transportation who was in charge of those kinds of things."

Greene continues: "We knew that what we had been working on—infrastructure protection—was about to go national, become a national security issue of significance. [Oklahoma City] was an event that was a catalyst for us to begin to think about terrorism in a different way."

## PRESIDENTIAL DECISION DIRECTIVE 39

On June 21, 1995, two months after the Oklahoma City bombing, President Clinton signed President Decision Directive 39 (PDD 39), "The U.S. Policy on Counterterrorism," assigning various anti-terrorism tasks to relevant agencies.[vi] Because of the sensitive nature of the twelve-page Directive, only a small portion was made public; the rest was classified.

Once again, an itemized review of the nation's infrastructure was called for. Under the six-point "Reduce Vulnerabilities" section of the PDD, the Department of Justice was charged with two important jobs. One was to evaluate the security of government offices and government installations and make recommendations about protecting them.

Says Jamie Gorelick, who was Deputy Attorney General at the time: "The Justice Department was given the role of reviewing the vulnerability to terrorism over all government facilities and that was run out of my office. It was done by the Marshal Service but with a lot of personal over-

**TIMELINE OF FEDERAL-LEVEL POLICYMAKING:** 1991 – 1995

1995—RAND Corporation, at the request of the Defense Department, conducted "The Day After…" simulation of an information warfare attack.

1995—PDD 39: The U.S. Counterterrorism Policy is signed by President Clinton. PDD 39 tasks the Attorney General with looking at vulnerabilities to critical national infrastructures.

**72** CRITICAL PATH

sight in my office. We went building by building of every federal facility of any sort—and there were thousands—with a vulnerability checklist. We had a review process and we determined down to each building level what they needed to do. . . .The State Department got all non-military facilities abroad and we got all the domestic. DOD got all the military personnel."

The second part of DOJ's responsibilities under PDD 39 was to create an interagency Cabinet-level group to examine infrastructure protection.[vii] The group's task was to identify critical infrastructures, the nature of threats against them, review existing mechanisms for protecting them, and review options for examining the problem in more depth.

PDD 39 had been drafted with input from DOJ and other agencies, so the assignment was not a surprise. Earlier, during the Directive drafting process, Gorelick—who had previously served as General Counsel at DOD—thought that DOD was better positioned than DOJ to handle "review of the vulnerability to terrorism of our critical national infrastructure." DOD, however, "wanted none of it," says Gorelick. "The Defense Department's basic reaction was 'We don't really want to get into this. We are doing our thing. We're going to protect our assets, that is, our military assets, and we have our affirmative capacities. . . and we think a broader conversation about . . .security actually has more danger to it than it has benefit and so we don't want to do it.' Now I don't know if those were the reasons, but those were the stated reasons."

Gorelick notes that "If the Defense Department wasn't going to do it, we [DOJ] were the obvious people to do it, the obvious institution to do it, but we had no real ability to do it."

DOJ had, in fact, been tasked since at least 1988 under E.O. 12656 with being the lead agency on aspects of planning for the physical protection of "essential resources and facilities." But Gorelick suggests that the department, specifically the FBI, "would often say that they wanted a set of responsibilities beyond solving bank robberies, but then they wouldn't do it. It wasn't valued. . . .[The FBI] didn't view its obligations as extending to real cooperation with the rest of the national security community and it resisted efforts to change."

After mulling over DOD's initial hands-off reaction, Gorelick crossed the Potomac again with a proposition for the Pentagon: "'If you won't take the lead on it, will you let us take the lead on it and you provide the relevant people from within the Department just to talk about what the next steps should be?' They said yes, and so we ended up with a working group of all the relevant parts of the government at a very interesting level."

## THE CRITICAL INFRASTRUCTURE WORKING GROUP

The Cabinet level members of the group included the Attorney General, the Director of the Central Intelligence Agency, the Deputy Secretary of Defense, the Deputy Attorney General, the Deputy Assistant to the President for National Security Affairs, the Vice President's National Security Advisor, and the Director of the FBI.[viii]

The principals were represented on a day-to-day basis by deputies. Gorelick chaired the group on behalf of Janet Reno. DOD sent Sheila G. Dryden, Principal Director for Emergency Preparedness Policy, Mary DeRosa, Associate Deputy General Counsel, and Brent Greene, Director for Infrastructure Policy. From the Office of the DCI (Central Intelligence Agency) came Jeffrey A. Benjamin. The White House sent Captain Richard J. Wilhelm, U.S. Navy and Military Advisor to the Vice President. DOJ supplied Michael A. Vatis, Associate Deputy Attorney General and Roger Pincus, Attorney-Advisor, Office of Intelligence Policy and Review. From the FBI came David V. Keyes, Chief of the Budget, Training and Analytical Division of the National Security Division.

Says Jim Kurtz, who was at DOD at the time: "It was a pretty remarkable affair . . . just the idea of the interagency [approach], being able to pull people together to look at a problem that way under the leadership of one department, that doesn't happen very often. [You can] witness the absolute disaster we've had in the transition in Iraq where the departments don't play nice together. It's always like a bunch of two-year-olds in a sandbox without enough toys to go around. You get different departments, each jealous of their turf, so I think the CIWG was a significant thing."[ix]

The Critical Infrastructure Working Group—or CIWG—as the interagency panel came to be called, followed a decision by the 'principals group' that "in light of the breadth of critical infrastructures and the multiplicity of sources and forms of attack, the Cabinet Committee should consider not only terrorist threats to the infrastructures, but also threats from other sources." The group expanded its inquiry to include cyber, not just physical attacks like those perpetrated on the World Trade Center and Murrah Building.

Says Jamie Gorelick: "You've got to give a tremendous amount of credit here to Janet Reno. She in particular started to see reports of individuals and groups using cyber means to do bad things. And the bad things could range from messing with the judge's credit card history as a way of intimidating him from sentencing a defendant to the malicious shutting down of 911 systems."

"There was a proliferation of information that started to build up about the use of cyber tools to steal money, intimidate people, [and] create mayhem generally," says Gorelick. "We also saw much more finished intelligence, if you will, that reflected nascent concerns that bad actors abroad might try to use the same set of cyber tools to possibly destroy our financial institutions, to shut down computer communications, etc."[x]

The previous three years had brought a few eye-opening cyber capers directly to the doorsteps of DOJ and DOD. In 1992, a hacker was able to penetrate Boeing's supercomputer, but was derailed before serious damage occurred. The FBI investigated and discovered that the perpetrator had also been able to access the passwords of a federal judge and a system administrator in the Federal Court in Seattle.

After the bombing of the Murrah Building in Oklahoma City (OK) in April 1995, Jamie Gorelick (center) and Senator Sam Nunn (center, left) were both instrumental in nudging the Clinton White House to create a Presidential Commission to explore critical infrastructure issues.

# Making the Connection: The Internet

Today's Internet can be traced to the late 1960s to a small, federally-funded research project undertaken by the Department of Defense's new Advanced Research Projects Agency (DARPA today). ARPA wanted to find a convenient way for its research community to connect and share information and data. The trick was to overcome the incompatibility of proprietary computer systems by sending data in a format that could be interpreted by different machines. ARPA researchers played with methods for breaking up data into small packets and sending them over communication links without tying up the line at the other end during transmission. The new method, called packet switching, permitted sharing of communication links, much as a mailbox can be used for multiple communications.

In September 1969, the ARPANET was born, followed quickly by an avalanche of follow-on technology designed to connect to ARPANET and to promote its usage. One of the most important developments was TCP/IP technology, deployed in 1983 as a method for allowing computers, particularly PC's, to use packet switching technology to ensure maximum data integrity or, more simply, to get a message from Point A to Point B without losing anything along the way.[1]

The original ARPANET exploded into complementary networks such as NSFNET and MILNET, the former used by the research and education community at large, the latter by the defense community. Usage of these new networks was theoretically restricted to their respective communities, but curiosity about the possibilities of regional and cross-country communication networks had been piqued. In 1988 commercial enterprises began developing private networks for use by the masses. The World Wide Web soon became a virtual community, complete with a host of benefits and dangers.

The original vision for a 'Galactic Network'[2] was not lost even as the Internet grew in usage and size. At its core, the Internet is still the original ARPANET—an open space connecting communities.

---

[1] TCP/IP (Transmission Control Protocol/Internet Protocol) is the basic communication language or protocol of the Internet. TCP/IP is a two-layer program. The higher layer, Transmission Control Protocol, manages the assembling of a message or file into smaller packets that are transmitted over the Internet and received by a TCP layer that reassembles the packets into the original message. The lower layer, Internet Protocol, handles the address part of each packet so that it gets to the right destination. Each gateway computer on the network checks this address to see where to forward the message. Even though some packets from the same message are routed differently than others, they'll be reassembled at the destination. Source: http://searchnetworking.techtarget.com/gDefinition/0,294236,sid7_gci214173,00.html

[2] Term used by J.C.R. Licklider of MIT who in 1962 envisioned a "globally interconnected set of computers through which everyone could quickly assess data and programs from any site." (www.isoc.org/oti/printversions/0797prleiner.html)

The so-called "Citibank Caper" in 1994 involved a Russian crime group that transferred $10 million out of Citibank accounts to different accounts in California, Finland, Israel, and Germany. The FBI was also involved in solving that case.

In 1994, two teenagers hacked into the computer network at an Air Force laboratory in Rome, New York. The incident cost the lab $500,000 to restore their computers and install security, a price tag that didn't reflect the cost of the data compromised. One of the two hackers pointed out— no doubt to DOD's chagrin— that .mil sites (i.e. military websites) were easier to hack into than other types of websites.[xi]

Initially, the CIWG's decision to add cyber met with a bit of derision: "I remember there were some people at the senior levels of government who thought it was a little bit too cute or a little bit too slang or trendy, and objected to it," says Vatis, "but we thought it had legs and stuck with it and it certainly has kept its legs."

The group also nailed down the categories of infrastructure that it felt needed to be reviewed. Drawing on 1988's Executive Order 12656, the CIWG identified eight categories of critical infrastructure:

- telecommunications;
- electrical power;
- gas and oil;
- banking and finance;
- transportation;
- water supply;
- emergency services;
- continuation of government

With a game plan in hand, the group began its deliberations.

"It was a bright, very experienced and diverse bunch," says Vatis, who chaired the meetings on behalf of his boss Gorelick. "[That] was part of the beauty of it. People came with very different backgrounds, very different experiences and very different views and yet it was relatively easy to come to consensus in defining the problem and in coming up with the recommendations. Now, there wasn't absolutely consensus on exactly how this all should be done . . . but it was fairly easy for us to reach consensus on the scope of the problem and the nature of it and what needed to be done at least in the very near term."

As part of its research process, the group was briefed by several people, including fellow member Greene. There was also plenty to draw on from what the departments themselves were up to. DOD had just finished conducting a series of "Day After" information warfare scenarios with the help of Rand Corporation. A major study by the Commission on Roles and Missions of the Armed Services (CORM) had underscored the value of reducing vulnerabilities in civilian infrastructures. And the CIA had just issued a groundbreaking classified report focused on attacks on SCADA networks.

The group's lifespan was "not long," says Vatis. "It was extremely quick actually given that it was government and inter-agency. . . .We came up with a recommendation that quickly was approved by the Deputy Attorney General and the Attorney General and then by the relevant Cabinet agency heads and then by the National Security Advisor and then by the President."

"When we were ready to pop out a recommendation," says Jamie Gorelick, "I went to the White House. I can't actually remember who I talked to. I said 'We've been burrowing away over here in this interagency process that we have just done on our own and unless you tell me not to, we're going to recommend to you a set of follow-on steps.' They said fine."

The CIWG "popped out" its report on February 6, 1996. After underscoring that threats come in two forms—physical and cyber—or a combination, the group made its two principal recommendations:

The first was to set up immediately, within the FBI, a small group that would keep an eye on infrastructure issues for the short term. Although the Infrastructure Protection Task Force (IPTF), as it was soon tagged, would later be criticized, its creators had known going in that what they were setting up was less than ideal.

Vatis had advocated quick action: "Let's do something that's workable even if it's not perfect. This was an urgent problem that needs to have a quick solution and we can't wait for the perfect solution."

The more "perfect solution" was, with luck, to come out of the group's second key recommendation: a full-time Presidential Commission devoted to looking at critical infrastructure. Such a policy group would "1) scope the problem, 2) review elements of the government and private sector contributing now to infrastructure assurance; 3) reach common ground in defining the threat; 4) determine legal and policy issues; 5) propose appropriate roles for government and industry in correcting deficiencies; and 6) propose national policy and legislative and regulatory changes."

Says Gorelick: "[This was] a problem that reached every government agency and every element of our economy, and it seemed to me that we needed to find facts, make our case and raise consciousness all at the same time, and thus, I thought a Presidential Commission would be the right way to do it."

It was important, noted the CIWG report, that major government stakeholders be represented by "full-time agency representatives" on the commission. And that the private sector needed to be included in the process—a stipulation that would become a key factor in the Commission's make-up and deliberations. There was also an interesting caveat that the commission "must appear to be a 'fair court' for reconciling significant national security, law enforcement, commercial and privacy concerns"—possibly a friendly warning that none of the players "in the sandbox" was to claim more "toys" than they were entitled to.

The tone of the final report was perhaps as important as its content: "No one was taking the role of Chicken Little," says David Keyes. "The outlook of the group was not the sky is falling, but rather we're beginning to see the potential that there are some cracks in the dam and we need to look at ways to shore it up."

The CIWG worked quickly and quietly, but its work had the intended effect: kicking to a higher level of visibility an issue that had been discussed mainly behind closed doors for a half century, and often only at a classified level. It was also an acknowledgment, perhaps, that the issue "wasn't ready to go," suggests Lee Zeichner, a consultant to the commission that evolved from the CIWG's work. "It needed to percolate a little bit more in the White House so they could get their arms around it and figure out how to manage it."

**TIMELINE OF FEDERAL-LEVEL POLICYMAKING: 1991 – 1995**

1995—Creation of the Critical Infrastructure Working Group (CIWG) under the Attorney General of the Department of Justice to examine threats to and vulnerabilities of critical national infrastructures. In addition to defining the infrastructures, the CIWG recommended further study by a presidential commission.

Zeichner points out that the "deep" issue of critical infrastructure attacks wasn't necessarily about just destruction, but included the specter of subtle disruption. "Look at the northeast blackout of 2003. How would you think about it if instead of two weeks, it was six months and how would you feel if it was six months and then it kept happening every three months in pockets. After a while, you would turn on the light but you'd think, 'Oh, is it going to go on?' So your mind set would change and it would change so much that you would behave differently. You would invest differently. The country would not be able to project as much power. That's critical infrastructure. The problem is, for the first time, the federal government cannot control a national security problem and that's deep, if you think about it. They can't bomb somewhere. They can't mobilize for war. They can't get the FBI stood up. And industry owns majority pieces of this."

Stevan Mitchell, who served as DOJ's representative on the Commission, agrees: "Up until that time, this whole [cyber] effort was not called infrastructure assurance or infrastructure protection. It was deep within the bowels of the Department of Defense. It was called Defensive Information Warfare and it was all highly classified and you couldn't talk about it at all. So one of the dramatic things that the CIWG did [and] that the Executive Order [E.O. 13010] did was say, 'Look, we need to shed some light on this. We need to talk publicly about it because a governmental solution, a classified solution, is not going to adequately safeguard our country's interests.' Furthermore, it can't be a solution set that is concocted by government and enacted by government. There has to be buy-in from the very beginning by the private sector and one way of assuring that from the very beginning is to have the private sector there full time, 50, 60 hours a week deliberating these solutions and making recommendations right alongside the public sector."

"And that's what happened," says Mitchell. "That's what the Executive Order called for and that's what the President's Commission on Critical Infrastructure Protection became. And I think it really was a tremendously important turning point in the history of how we address this as a policy matter for our nation.

[i] Kupperman wasn't referring specifically to computer worms and viruses, but the comment was prescient. In 1978 the first worm was developed at PARC Xerox by John Shoch and Jon Hupp during their experiments on mobile software. They took the name from the tapeworm monster in John Brunner's novel The Shockwave Rider.

[ii] Congressional Record, 26 February 1990: S1642 or <http://leahy.senate.gov/press/200002/00029b.html>.

[iii] W. B. Latta, A More Effective Army Through Electronic Data Processing Systems (Washington: Industrial College of the Armed Forces, April 1957, Thesis No. 74) 3.

[iv] From the Lane Report: " In January 1986, NSC issued NSDD 207 which directed FEMA, under the auspices of the Interdepartmental Group on Terrorism, to identify the extent to which various critical infrastructure elements (e.g. the computerized banking system, power grids, and communications networks) were vulnerable to terrorism and propose near and long term solutions." (Lane 87.)

[v] Details of the Murrah building bombing: At 9:02 a.m., a Ryder rental truck packed with explosives blew out a 30-foot wide, 8-foot deep crater on the front of the building, killing 169 people, including 19 children, and injuring more than 500.

[vi] PDD 39 specifically directed the Secretary of Transportation to "reduce vulnerability affecting the security of airports in the United States."

[vii] PDD 39 required the Attorney General to "chair a Cabinet Committee to review the vulnerability to terrorism of government facilities and critical national infrastructure and make recommendations to [the President] and the appropriate Cabinet member or Agency head."

[viii] Principals of the Critical Infrastructure Working Group: Janet Reno; John Deutsch (Dir of CIA); John White, Deputy Secretary of Defense; Samuel R. Berger, Deputy Assistant to the President for National Security Affairs; Leon Fuerth, Assistant to the VP for National Security Affairs; Louis J. Freeh, Director, FBI.

[ix] The debacle that accompanied FEMA's formation in 1979 is another example.

[x] The CIWG was not alone in pondering the ramifications of cyber. For example, the NSIE—National Security Information Exchange—had been created in 1991 as a sub-committee of the National Security Telecommunications Advisory Committee to explore vulnerabilities and electronic intrusions. The NSTAC had been established earlier by President Ronald Reagan by Executive Order 12382 to gather industry executives from the major telecom service providers, finance, aerospace and information technology companies to provide industry-based advice to the President on implementing national security and emergency preparedness in communications policy. Tensions between the U.S. and the U.S.S.R. were an historic high when Reagan created the NSTAC.

[xi] Richard Power, "Joy Riders: Mischief That Leads to Mayhem," Informit.com (30 October 2000) <http://www.informit.com/articles/article.asp?p=19603>.

Souvenir t-shirts from the 2003 blackout in New York City.

# CHAPTER 6

# A Great Debate:

## The Deliberations of the President's Commission on Critical Infrastructure Protection

*"We weren't blinded by the Soviet threat anymore. We were seeing these other threats. Those groups, because of our cyber dependence, now had a way of attacking the nation without ever encountering the nation's defense forces.…You couldn't fly a bomber at the United States without encountering a radar warning system. You couldn't fire a missile at the United States, anywhere in the world, without encountering a space-based detection capability. You could, however, launch what we called a logic bomb. There are all kinds of names for them, but you could launch an attack, a cyber attack, without ever encountering anything except the public switch network, the Internet, and the World Wide Web."*

Phil Lacombe
President's Commission on Infrastructure Protection
Oral History Interview

After the Critical Infrastructure Working Group (CIWG) issued its recommendations in February 1996, events continued to unfold that seemed to underscore the timeliness of the group's recommendations. In late June, a large blast rocked Khobar Towers, a U.S. compound in a military facility in Dhahran, Saudi Arabia. Closer to home, the Department of Defense's CERT at Carnegie Mellon reported to Congress that it had recently closed 350 computer intrusion cases—but opened 500 new ones.

Congress was busy too. Senators John Glenn and Sam Nunn were holding hearings in May, June and July, including two on the subject of "Security in Cyberspace."

On the agenda for one of the Glenn-Nunn hearings was the General Accounting Office's new report, "Information Security: Computer Attacks at DOD Post Increasing Risks."

The executive summary of the GAO's report delivered the bad news:

The exact number of attacks cannot be readily determined because only a small portion are actually detected and reported. However, Defense Information Systems Agency (DISA) data implies that Defense may have experienced as many as 250,000 attacks last year. DISA information also shows that attacks are successful 65 percent of the time, and that the number of attacks is doubling each year, as Internet use increases along with the sophistication of "hackers" and their tools.

At a minimum, these attacks are a multimillion dollar nuisance to Defense. At worst, they are a serious threat to national security. Attackers have seized control of entire Defense systems, many of which support critical functions, such as weapons systems research and development, logistics, and finance. Attackers have also stolen, modified, and destroyed data and software. In a well-publicized attack on Rome Laboratory, the Air Force's premier command and control research facility, two hackers took control of laboratory support systems, established links to foreign Internet sites, and stole tactical and artificial intelligence research data.[i]

The potential for catastrophic damage is great. Organized foreign nationals or terrorists could use "information warfare" techniques to disrupt military operations by harming command and control systems, the public switch network, and other systems or networks Defense relies on. Defense is taking action to address this growing problem, but faces significant challenges in controlling unauthorized access to its computer systems. Currently, Defense is attempting to react to successful attacks as it learns of them, but it has no uniform policy for assessing risks, protecting its systems, responding to incidents, or assessing damage.

Two months before the GAO testified at the Glenn-Nunn hearings, the CIWG had distilled its recommendations into the form of a draft

Executive Order for consideration by the President. Then the wait began. One member of the CIWG recalls that "time went by and time went by and time went by" before anything happened.

"It had stalled," says Jamie Gorelick flatly. "We weren't making the progress that we needed to make. . . . I can't give you the specifics [but] I think that Sam Nunn finally said, 'I keep hearing people saying that they're going to address this issue and they're not, so I'm going to have a hearing' . . . I went back to the National Security Council and said, 'You'd better pop this out [i.e. the Executive Order]' and as I recall, I was able in my testimony to address it."

Executive Order 13010 was signed on July 15, 1996, less than 24 hours before Gorelick appeared at the Glenn-Nunn hearings. The Executive Order gave the green light to both the interim Infrastructure Protection Task Force (IPTF) and the President's Commission on Critical Infrastructure Protection (PCCIP)—the two key provisions of the CIWG's recommendations.

The substance of EO 13010 was brief and to the point. After echoing the CIWG's eight categories of vulnerable CI, it sketched out the general problem:

*"Threats to these critical infrastructures fall into two categories: physical threats to tangible property ("physical threats"), and threats of electronic, radio-frequency, or computer-based attacks on the information or communications components that control critical infrastructures ("cyber threats"). Because many of these critical infrastructures are owned and operated by the private sector, it is essential that the government and private sector work together to develop a strategy for protecting them and assuring their continued operation."*

The Executive Order then laid out the new commission's mission:
SEC. 4. MISSION. The Commission shall:
(a) within 30 days of this order, produce a statement of its mission objectives, which will elaborate the general objectives set forth in this order, and a detailed schedule for addressing each mission objective, for approval by the Steering Committee;
(b) identify and consult with:[i] elements of the public and private sectors that conduct, support, or contribute to infrastructure assurance;[ii] owners and operators of the critical infrastructures; and[iii]

other elements of the public and private sectors, including Congress, that have an interest in critical infrastructure assurance issues and that may have differing perspectives on these issues;

(c) assess the scope and nature of the vulnerabilities of, and threats to, critical infrastructures;

(d) determine what legal and policy issues are raised by efforts to protect critical infrastructures and assess how these issues should be addressed;

(e) recommend a comprehensive national policy and implementation strategy for protecting critical infrastructures from physical and cyber threats and assuring their continued operation;

(f) propose any statutory or regulatory changes necessary to effect its recommendations; and

(g) produce reports and recommendations to the Steering Committee as they become available; it shall not limit itself to producing one final report.

## STANDING UP THE COMMISSION

While the interim Information Protection Task Force (IPTF) set up shop at the FBI, the process of setting up a presidential commission got underway.

The small group that put together the Executive Order had spent part of the effort wrestling with the question of the commission's composition. Brent Greene, who was named to the PCCIP as the representative from DOD, recalls that determining the scale of the enterprise was one of the first items on the group's agenda: "Most commissions have five to six people who are absolute icons in their field or in name recognition or what-have-you, but we were dealing with a different kind of animal."

The "animal" needed to have as much across-the-board representation from agencies as practicable. Without broad participation, buy-ins down the line would be few and far between. On the other hand, it quickly became clear that a line needed to be drawn:

"We started talking about…agency representation," says Greene. "So, do you bring every agency in? Oh, boy, you could be talking 20 agencies, 25 agencies, 10 agencies. How many agencies do you want? What are the big ones? In retrospect, I think we made a major mistake in that I think we should've had State Department there…. Some of them were no-brainers. CIA, FBI, DOD, NSA, Commerce, Transportation, Energy. We

General Robert T. "Tom" Marsh left a job in the private sector to chair the President's Commission on Critical Infrastructure Protection. Although initially "somewhat reluctant" to take the post, Marsh considered it his duty to take on the assignment when asked by the White House.

decided to stop at 10."

The others were FEMA, Department of Justice, and Treasury.

The Executive Order also stipulated that each agency could have two representatives, one of whom "may be an individual from outside the government who shall be employed by the agency on a full-time basis." In other words, each public sector representative could have a private sector counterpart.

That brought the permissible Commission membership to twenty. But even so large a number wasn't the end of the appointment process. The Executive Order had laid out layers of review that added nearly three dozen others to the mix. A Principals Committee was to be set up to "review any reports or recommendations before submission to the President." Its membership was composed of the heads of the ten agencies represented on the Commission, plus three others. Working on behalf of the Principals Committee was a Steering Committee, composed of the Commission's Chairman and four top government officials. The four included: Janet Reno, Attorney General; John J. Hamre, Deputy Secretary of Defense; Donald Kerrick, Deputy Assistant to the President for National Security Affairs; and Don Gips, Deputy Assistant to the Vice President for National Security Affairs.

Finally, an Advisory Committee of industry leaders was to be appointed by the President to provide the perspective of infrastructure owners and operators. Sam Nunn and Jamie Gorelick were to serve as co-chair of the Committee. Fifteen others joined them.

In anticipation of the arrival of such a large number of Commissioners, plus staff, a few early arrivals to the Commission began scouting for space. Initially, a berth near or in the White House complex seemed desirable, "but it turns out those kinds of spaces are hard to get," says Irv Pikus, the Commission's representative from Commerce.

What at first was a disappointment turned out to have an upside. Somewhat ironically, the Executive Branch wasn't set up "to support all of the IT connectivity that's become so core to what we needed to do," Pikus notes. "[T]he White House spaces weren't wired for the kind of bandwidth connectivity that we needed."

Instead, space in a building in nearby Rosslyn, Virginia, was made available, with enough room to allow the Commission to expand and eventually take up an entire floor. The agency to which the Rosslyn building belonged was DOD. The Pentagon had agreed to play host to the Commission by housing it in DOD facilities and supplying the logistical necessities.

"DOD would pay all the bills, provide the space, provide the staff support, administrative, security and all that," says Phil Lacombe. "So you really had a DOD-supported presidential commission."

"[DOD was] very, very good about it," says General Robert "Tom" Marsh, who chaired the Commission. "The Commission had been stood up, but none of the infrastructure had been put in place to support it, so DOD gave us a place out of one of their facilities. They put us in their budget and gave us funding citations to use. We were up and running even though . . . I hadn't been officially appointed or anything else."

The relative ease with which a home base was secured even before the Commission's head was appointed would turn out to be one of the few logistical questions to be answered quickly.

TIMELINE OF FEDERAL-LEVEL POLICYMAKING: 1996

**1996 February**—Information Technology Reform Act required government agencies to appoint a chief information officer (CIO) and become more information technology oriented in their delivery of services. Also known as the Clinger-Cohen Act.

**1996 April**—the U.S. Treasury created FinCEN, the Financial Crime Enforcement Network. The FinCEN requires financial institutions to report suspicious activity and intrusions. Institutions that do not comply are subject to a $5000 penalty.

A few of the ten federal agencies that were to be part of the Commission moved quickly to select representatives. Brent Greene (DOD), David Keyes (FBI), Dave Jones (DOE), Irv Pikus (Commerce) and John Powers (FEMA) were among the earliest to arrive. [See Appendix C for full list of PCCIP.]

Greene notes that "in some cases we tried to shape where [appointments] were going. Tom Falvey, for example, had worked for me in the Infrastructure Protection Directorate...so I specifically said, 'Hey, - [Department of] Transportation—you may want to think about Tom Falvey.' It wasn't a matter of, 'Where is there a senior executive who's available?' We said, 'Where is somebody who gets it, who understands the underlying issues?'"

While the agencies sorted out the question of selecting their representatives, Marsh pushed to get things moving on other fronts. The Commission had been given only a year in which to produce its report, so every minute counted. Marsh called on Phil Lacombe, who had served as Special Assistant to the Chairman of the recently-completed Commission on the Roles and Missions of the Armed Forces (CORM), to help jump-start matters, including the mission statement required within thirty days by the White House. Lacombe took two weeks from his job at the Aerospace Education Foundation to get the ball rolling. He had hardly said goodbye, when Marsh called him back to join the Commission full-time as Staff Director. Lacombe agreed.

"I think I brought Phil Lacombe on without any authority of any kind," says Marsh. "'Come and go to work, and then somehow we'll figure out how to let the paperwork catch up.'"

Both men quickly discovered that "paperwork" promised to be a major chokepoint for getting the Commission up and running.

"There were some assumptions made," says Lacombe. "Like you could appoint the Commission staff quickly. You could appoint the commissioners quickly. You could do all that stuff.... Of course, that all turned out to be not true."

Using the "let the paperwork catch up" mantra, Marsh and Lacombe plunged into finding staff as quickly as possible.

Jim Kurtz, who had functioned in the role of Chief of Staff of the CORM with Lacombe, remembers his interview with Marsh as a fast-moving blur. "In the last five minutes, he said, 'I want you to be Chief of Staff.'" Kurtz demurred over the title, but signed on.

"We had to twist the policy community's arm to get them to let him go," says Lacombe. "He had just gone into a new job at DOD [on the Joint Staff's Director for Strategic Plans and Policy.] But they let him go."

Another fast recruit was the Commission's General Counsel: "The Air Force ponied up a guy named Bob Giovagnoni who is an Air Force colonel and had been the general counsel at the Office of Special Investigations," says Lacombe. "Giovagnoni came because he had a high interest in cyber security and cyber law. Kurtz came for the challenge of doing the charter, the task of the Commission. We also went after a guy named Brian Hoey, an Air Force lieutenant colonel. [He was] a public affairs officer who had worked with me years before. General Marsh was going to need an executive officer, someone who would make sure that the scheduling and those things were done by the secretaries and admin folks. But more importantly, to be a content-oriented executive officer, [who] would understand the issues and could be sort of a one-person special staff for Marsh."

In time, the staff of the Commission would fill out to about seventy-five people. But at the start, says Kurtz, it was a bare bones operation. "It was a fledgling start-up.... You've got a lot of people who are eager to get started to work and you don't have the wherewithal to do it. There is no computer network set up. You don't have outside communications. You don't have any routines at all. Any office you go to over time develops routines and if somebody new comes into it, they learn that routine. They might change it over time. We didn't have any routines. Everybody came in with their own routines...so there's always a lot of confusion and friction at the beginning. The commissioners, as they were called, the people from other federal agencies, were coming in and that was a slow process to get them installed."

Appointments trickled in from the agencies. Part of the slowness, says Bill Joyce, Commissioner from the CIA, was attributable to the fact that "especially in the early days, the Commission was not looked at as a particularly worthwhile position.... Commissions in general are not necessarily highly regarded. Sometimes they are; sometimes they're not.... These are really, really tough issues...[Critical infrastructure protection] is a tough area to work in."

That the Commission wasn't being formed in the immediate wake of a tragedy also lent an amorphous air to its mission. Although the Commission was inspired in part by the bombings of 1993 and 1995, it wasn't set up to investigate those particular events. Its mission was more nebulous, less "sexy" than delving into a headline-generating crisis.

Says Brent Greene: "The Commission was absolutely unique in that most commissions are established in response to something horrible happening. TWA 800 goes down. Vice President Gore establishes a Presidential Commission on Aviation Safety and Security. Something bad happens. Now you get a presidential commission. Now you go do it. We established the President's Commission for Critical Infrastructure Protection but nobody had attacked critical infrastructure yet. We were ahead of our time."

Recruiting from the private sector turned out to be no easier—in fact, perhaps more difficult—than finding representatives from the government. Marsh knew a "little bit about recruiting people, [but] I had no idea how difficult this was going to be. At first, it looked so simple. We wanted to be half private sector and half public sector. Gee, that's neat, but then when we started to get into it, how you could possibly get these people from industry to come into government? That was one challenge, just to persuade somebody to do that, to leave their company and then go back a year later or a year and a half later."

"I tried to tell them that we'd been formed up as a President's Commission and we had a very, very important mission," continues Marsh. "We didn't want the outcome of this to be government-centric but …balanced, with the interest of the public and the private sector, and [so] it was very much in their interest to have somebody on this Commission. We put it that way…[but] we weren't as successful as I had hoped we would be. On the other hand, we were racing head to the wall and we couldn't spend full time on recruiting. Things were moving and moving fast."

Fast—up to a point. Marsh soon discovered that despite the Clinton administration mandate to complete the Commission's work within

**1996 (June–July)**—'Security in Cyberspace' hearings conducted by the Senate Government Affairs Subcommittee on Permanent Investigations.

**1996 July**—Executive Order 13010 created the President's Commission on Critical Infrastructure Protection (PCCIP) and the Infrastructure Protection Task Force (IPTF).

twelve months, the White House itself was frustratingly slow about signing off on Commission appointments. Marsh's own appointment turned out to be one of the most dragged-out affairs of the entire Commission.

By his own account, he had been "somewhat reluctant" to take up the invitation to head the Commission. Just a year earlier he had settled into a full-time position as Director of the Air Force Aid Society, the official charity of the Air Force. But Marsh had what he called a "typical military reaction" to the call to duty: "If this has to be done, we'll do it." He checked with the Trustees of the AFAS, who agreed to a one-year leave of absence. Some of his contemporaries told him point blank: "You're nuts," but Marsh agreed to the post anyway.

Besides feeling the tug of duty, Marsh found the subject of critical infrastructure interesting. He had had some exposure to the issue twenty years earlier. "When I commanded the electronic systems division up at Hanscom Air Force Base (Massachusetts) for four years, we had the responsibility for what's referred to as the C4I— the command, control, communications, computer intelligence systems—for the Air Force. We became very much aware as we developed those systems...of their vulnerabilities.... We knew we were putting things together in a sort of a haphazard fashion, that we weren't spending as much time, energy and effort as we should have on the vulnerability of those systems."

"We recognized that we were creating what you might call critical nodes," continues Marsh. "That is, so many things had to be interfaced at critical points either in the airplanes, [such as] the command and control airplanes like AWACS or Joint Stars, that we realized that if you knock out those critical nodes, you could lose your entire system. So we were constantly thinking about what kind of back-up could we have, and back-up wasn't easy and practical in many cases. That was the kind of vulnerability we saw. We saw the jamming vulnerability...and tried to make our sys-

**TIMELINE OF FEDERAL-LEVEL POLICYMAKING: 1996**

**1996 July**—Infrastructure Protection Task Force (IPTF) set up within the Department of Justice to increase "the coordination of existing infrastructure protection efforts in order to better address, and prevent, crises that would have a debilitating regional or national impact."[1]

**1996 July**—Executive Order 13011, signed by President Clinton, created Chief Information Officer positions at all executive agencies, including the federal CIO Council, and required agencies to improve information technology management.

[1] See footnote, page 97 sidebar.

tems as resistant as possible to jamming type interference. But we hadn't yet come into the computer vulnerability as such, viruses and so on. As I took over command of the entire Air Force Systems Command (1981–1984), which had responsibility for all the computerized systems, I still was impressed with the vulnerability of systems."

Marsh responded quickly to the White House's invitation to head the President's Commission on Critical Infrastructure Protection, but his appointment was not finalized until Christmas Eve of 1996. "I was in limbo all that time, but working full-time every day…on Commission business."

Appointments to the Advisory Committee fared no better, to the point that the Commission had nearly finished its work in 1997 before the group was fully constituted. "The Advisory Committee came together very, very late," says Marsh. "In fact, too late. And so that was really more of what you might want to call [a] showcase."

Kurtz agrees: "Horrid, horrid delays in getting people [vetted]. We went through such agony trying to get an Advisory Committee name[d].... The goal was to have those big well-known Wall Street industry kinds of names put their seal of approval on this whole thing, but…we'd submit a list of names and nothing would happen. The White House General Counsel's office…could not get their act straight. They had other things on their mind [i.e. the Monica Lewinsky scandal]. It never seemed to be a priority to get it done."

## FULL SPEED AHEAD

One result of the slow pace of appointments was the need for a three-month extension. "All of the pieces of the Commission" weren't put together until February 1997, says Lacombe. The final report was due in July. The Executive Order was amended to allow for the extra three months.

Marsh wasn't happy: "I figured I'd been asked to do this and it's a year long. By any means, I'm not going to extend this thing. We're going to get it done on time and no excuse. Put our head down and just go like hell."

Some things, however, couldn't be done until Marsh's own appointment was finalized. The Commission lacked the authority, for example, to conduct public hearings until the Chairman was made official. While awaiting White House sign-off, "we concentrated in the early part of the process on doing the infrastructure research, the Sector Reports," says

Lacombe. "As we got all the pieces in place, we went on to the actual issue identification and fleshing out what we knew based on the public hearings."

One of the early pieces involved figuring out how to ensure that the Commission's deliberations would not be subject to federal Freedom of Information Act (FOIA) regulations. The PCCIP was going to be looking at the "under belly" of CI and wanted to be sure that sensitive data reviewed by the Commission was not going to inadvertently turn into publicly available information. The Commission's general counsel Bob Giovagnoni crafted the necessary language and process to be sure that Commission fell under the Presidential Records Act. He also worked with DOD and NSA to come up with a classification guide for handling classified material examined by the Commission.

Despite the assorted administrative challenges, the Commissioners followed Marsh's lead and dove into their assignment as soon as possible.

## DIVIDING UP THE WORLD

One task that seemed both logical and timely was reviewing the eight CI categories identified by the CIWG, and deciding whether to follow that particular structure. The job fell initially to the few public sector commissioners who had been able to get assigned to the Commission relatively quickly, including Greene, Pikus, Joe Moorcones (NSA), Jones, Stevan Mitchell (DOJ), and Powers.

The group considered whether eight categories were sufficient and at first thought no. "We talked about agriculture and food…and whether or not we should expand our charter," says Jones. But the group realized that the eight initially suggested were "a lot on our plate" and decided not to stray beyond.

Mitchell explains with humor that the early deliberations naturally focused on the agency turf represented by the first batch to arrive.

"Whenever you get…different government agencies around a table to talk about a problem, the immediate temptation is to begin to divide the problem and the solutions along jurisdictional lines roughly reflecting those agencies' interests. So, naturally the intelligence folks were looking at it from an intelligence perspective and thinking of intelligence-based solutions. Me, as the Justice guy, was looking at it from a legal perspective and on down the line."

Then, the private sector representatives began to arrive. One by one, their eyebrows went up when they discovered what their public sector counterparts had been doing. Their reaction, no doubt, was similar to the dismay the private sector had felt in reading the industrial mobilization plans that the War Department had cooked up between World War I and World War II.

Says Mitchell: "They would say, 'Hold on a second, you guys, you're dividing up the world according to your agency's jurisdiction, but guess what? You don't own the world; 95 percent of the infrastructure that you guys are trying to divvy up and talk about are out there in the private sector. We need to go about this in radically different ways.'

"I would venture to say that probably 90 to 99 percent of the preliminary thinking and the preliminary work that we had done as government representatives was quickly tossed out the window in favor of a much more trying, much more challenging, but ultimately much more productive and universally acceptable way of addressing the problem process-wise. It was very funny."

The result of the second round of discussion was a collapsing of the original eight categories of the EO into five "sectors":

- **Information & Communications** (telecommunications, computers and software, Internet, satellites, fiber optics)
- **Physical Distribution** (railroads, air traffic, maritime, intermodal, pipelines)
- **Energy** (electrical power, natural gas, petroleum, production, distribution, storage)
- **Banking & Finance** (financial transactions, stock and bond markets, Federal Reserve)
- **Vital Human Services** (water, emergency services, government services)

TIMELINE OF FEDERAL-LEVEL POLICYMAKING: 1996

1996 October—National Institute of Standards and Technology created the Federal Computer Incident Response Capability (FedCIRC), to provide all civilian government agencies the ability to offer computer security training, emergency support and vulnerability assessments.

Says Irv Pikus, "I'm not sure why we figured those five, but actually that conversation was led by [Joe] Moorcones. I thought he made a good case for doing it the way we did it, so there was energy and banking/finance and telecommunications/information, and transportation. [Transportation] became known as physical distribution. . . . And vital human services, which was sort the grab bag of everything. It was stuff that we couldn't fit into any other category."

As the Commission began working together, it became clear that the members brought not only varying perspectives, but different levels of understanding about critical infrastructure.

"Probably less than half came in understanding critical infrastructure protection issues," says Greene. "And that's okay, because we got a bunch of people with a whole lot of experience, but we [also] got a whole bunch of other people that were bringing totally fresh thinking to the challenge."

People also brought agendas, especially those Commissioners who were representing their federal employers. "There was a little bit of jockeying among the agencies," says Lacombe. "Justice didn't want DOD to be in charge. Commerce didn't want DOD to be in charge. Nobody wanted Justice to be in charge. . . . If you ask what the interest of the different agencies or constituencies might have been at the time, you'd have to conclude that when the Commission was set up, I think there were those in the Department of Justice who really thought that the whole purpose of the Commission was to take a look at this and then conclude that there was clearly a need for more FBI agents and more FBI agents with more technical training. I think DOD hoped that they wouldn't get stuck with the bill. I think Commerce hoped that it would have a role in NIST [National Institute of Standards and Technology] or something to set standards or any role that they could get."

## DEFINING THE SCOPE: PHYSICAL VERSUS CYBER

Although the PCCIP's charter didn't stipulate how to apportion time between the two categories of threats—physical or cyber—the group elected to put its energy into the latter. Marsh characterized the choice as a fairly simple one: he didn't think that the group could contribute much to the existing knowledge base of how to handle physical threats. Cyber, on the other hand, was "an emerging new threat." Time was a factor, too: "None of us wanted to turn this into a life's work," says Nancy Wong, the private sector Commissioner invited by NSA. "[So] we decided to pick an

# Infrastructure Protection Task Force

In addition to creating the President's Commission on Critical Infrastructure Protection (PCCIP), Executive Order 13010—issued by the White House in July 1995—created an "interim coordinating mission" to address infrastructure protection while the PCCIP deliberated and issued recommendations for a formal, comprehensive policy. The Infrastructure Protection Task Force (IPTF) was chaired by the FBI on the grounds that computer intrusions often require research to determine actual intent. The FBI already possessed authority to investigate intrusions to determine whether an attack was criminal, recreational or a national security threat.[1]

The IPTF was a multi-agency task force responsible for reducing infrastructure vulnerabilities by: providing threat and warning information; analyzing intelligence and detecting potential attacks; providing education and training on infrastructure assurance; determining the nature of attacks – criminal, foreign attack, recreational hacker or network failure; and coordinating information sharing within the federal government and private sector.

Around the same time that the IPTF was established, the FBI created the Computer Investigations and Infrastructure Threat Assessment Center (CIITAC) in response to an up-tick in computer crimes. It was thought that CIITAC's "watch and respond"[2] capabilities would be able to provide the new IPTF with valuable support.

Acquiring resources, budget and personnel proved difficult for the IPTF and hampered its ability to respond in more than an ad hoc fashion to infrastructure attacks. As a result, the IPTF was replaced by the National Infrastructure Protection Center (NIPC) in February 1998.

---

[1] Vatis, Michael (Director, National Infrastructure Protection Center, FBI). "Testimony on National Infrastructure Protection before the Senate Judiciary Subcommittee on Terrorism, Technology and Government Information, June 10, 1998 .
[2] Ibid., 1998

area which no one was addressing."

The cyber focus soon led to the Commission being dubbed the "Cyber Commission," somewhat to the frustration of its members, who felt that the moniker was dismissive or misleading. They point out that physical threats were factored into the group's work, but simply accorded less emphasis. Among the incidents that the Commission took a look at was the Tokyo sarin gas attack the year before, which killed twelve and affected thousands of other subway commuters. The group was also keenly aware of the bombing at the Olympics in Atlanta that happened just as the Commission was getting organized.[ii]

Having gravitated to an emphasis on cyber, the group needed to get up to speed on Information Age technology.

"There was a major effort to get everybody up to the same level of awareness," says David Keyes, Commissioner from the FBI. Howard Schmidt, the Chief of Information Security at Microsoft, came in more than once to talk to the group. "While many of these Commissioners knew their business very well," explains a Commission staff member, "they did not understand computers and I don't know that any of them ever really did truly understand computers at the level I think they needed to understand it. But they did get a good grasp of a lot of the security issues that were going on."

Another early task was ensuring that everyone was speaking the same language, especially in defining critical infrastructure. The group had the "official" definition from Executive Order 13010, of course—"those systems essential to the minimum operations of the economy and government"—but putting it into terms that everyone could readily grasp was important . . . and difficult.

"One of the greatest challenges was: What is this infrastructure? Tell me what the financial infrastructure of the United States is?" says Marsh. "Is it something I can touch? Can somebody put it up here on the board? We talk about this critical infrastructure but do we know what we're talking about? . . . . A great effort was put into defining the systems and once you define the systems, then defining their vulnerabilities."

"We had a lot of discussions [about] how critical is the banking and finance industry to the survival of the United States," says Lacombe. "Pretty damned critical. But any one bank? Is the infrastructure that supports any one bank critical? No. We've seen very large banks disappear off the face of the earth and we've all continued."

Nailing down the universe of potential threats to infrastructure was another major exercise. It required "thinking differently"—a phrase destined to become both a Commission theme and the subtitle of one of the PCCIP's main publications.[iii]

"It was a different kind of threat than everybody was used to," says Kurtz. "The threat we all grew up with was Soviet tanks and airplanes that our satellites could count and we knew how big they were and we could read their mail and so forth. We all had the sense of what the threat was. Well, now, it was a much more amorphous threat that could do great harm to us. And what it could do harm to was not necessarily just military establishments; it could do harm to the economy; it could do harm to our way of life by curtailing our freedoms or whatever."

"When you want to stop bad things from happening," says Lacombe, "that means pushing farther and farther away . . . out from the shore. That's what we did. We have fought all major wars on someone else's turf. We've pushed our defense across those oceans. Once we realized that we were subject to cyber attack, there are no oceans, there are no boundaries. So we really had a lot of fundamental concepts that had to be reevaluated."

The Commission developed a list of what it felt constituted the universe of likely threats. They ranged from accidents and natural disasters, to the machinations of industrial saboteurs, hackers, and foreign intelligence operations. [Note: For full list, see Chapter Seven]

Commission members next sorted themselves into teams to cover the five sectors that had been identified early on. Depending upon the type of expertise they brought to the table, some Commissioners worked on several sector teams, formally or informally. Mary Culnan of Georgetown University, for example, brought a specialization in privacy issues that proved useful when discussing the public's right to know versus the value or expediency of withholding sensitive information. Another Commission member—Stevan Mitchell from DOJ—supplied the legal backdrop to discussions involving potential changes to existing law and regulations.

"One of the real challenges of the Commission's work was that all of these different infrastructure sectors are regulated both to different degrees and in very different ways," says Mitchell. "The water infrastructure is historically regulated in a very, very local way—in a hands-on, but very local way. The banking sector is regulated in a much more federalized way, a much more nationalized way, at least with respect to the federal financial institutions."

## MASTERING THE LEGAL LANDSCAPE

Recognizing that the Commission needed to understand the underlying legal framework in order to offer relevant recommendations for tweaking it, Mitchell set out to map the "legal landscape" with a team of consultants and law students. In spite of the government's notorious penchant for studying, it was a monumental task that no one had ever tackled.

"One of the very first things we did was try to get a handle on the authorities that were already existing within the federal agencies that could potentially be used to enhance infrastructure assurance," explains Mitchell. "Before we were able to do that, it required us to back pedal a couple of steps. First of all, [we had to] come up with a definition of what the heck we possibly meant by infrastructure assurance since it's not really easy to walk up to general counsel of some agency and say, 'By the way, what are your infrastructure assurance authorities?' You'd get kicked out of that office pretty quickly, and so we had to spell that out."

"We had to describe exactly what it was we were looking for and then we had to motivate these folks [representatives of general counsel's offices] to actually go and do some research for us," continues Mitchell. "So [we] convened a couple of meetings of representatives of general counsel's offices. . . . We briefed them on what our Commission's mission was, what kinds of things we were looking for, what we meant by infrastructure assurance. For example, legal authorities that helped to make infrastructure less vulnerable to destruction or attack or to make infrastructure harms to a lesser degree in the event of a destruction or attack, or that would make it readily reconstituted to reestablish vital capabilities. And then we identified the individual infrastructures we were interested in . . . including telecommunications, electric power, gas and oil storage, banking and finance, transportation, water supply systems, emergency services, continuity of government operations, etc. We laid out this in a matrix and we collected this information from the counsel's offices."

It wasn't always easy. Some agencies offered up blank stares when asked for their input. Others required substantial "hand-holding" to cough up the requested information. The exercise was enlightening, if only for what it revealed about many agencies' cognizance of critical infrastructure issues.

In the end, Mitchell was able to get what he wanted, thanks in large part to his team of consultants who pored over the federal criminal code and code of federal regulations and pulled out anything that appeared to be relevant to infrastructure. "There are literally fifty, sixty volumes to the federal criminal code," says Mitchell, "each a different title, each containing statutes and laws that are constructed by the courts in ways that might not be readily apparent. It was a fantastically huge undertaking."

The final product of months of furiously conducted research through thousands of pages of laws and regulations was a searchable CD of legal authorities covering every aspect of infrastructure. Mitchell was able to circulate it to all of the Commissioners: "Here's the toolkit . . . . Take [it] into account in your deliberations."

---

<sup>i</sup> This is the Rome Labs incident mentioned in Chapter Four.

<sup>ii</sup> The Atlanta bombing took place on July 27, 1996.

<sup>iii</sup> Critical Foundations: Thinking Differently. The publication served as an executive summary of the larger PCCIP report, Critical Foundations: Protecting America's Infrastructure. The excerpts in this chapter are from Thinking Differently.

The PCCIP's public outreach included a series of site hearings around the country to which businesses, associations, government officials and individuals were invited to enlighten the Commission on issues and concerns related to infrastructure security.

# CHAPTER 7

# Thinking Differently:

## Inverting the National Security Pyramid

*A wide variety of measures are available to prevent or correct network disruptions; but they are expensive and several strong economic and cultural pressures resist corrective action despite the serious nature of the threat. Nothing less than a program of national proportions can succeed in overcoming these deep-seated disincentives.*

"America's Hidden Vulnerabilities:
Crisis Management in a Society of Networks."
Center for Strategic and International Studies, 1984

S ector teams fanned out to conduct public meetings and make on-site visits to gather insights into specific infrastructure issues. Marsh had concluded that the wisest course of action was simply to tell the White House what he was doing, rather than wait for a green light. Sandy Berger, National Security Advisor at the time, was kept informed of the Commission's outreach efforts, and was, in Marsh's words, "supportive, in the sense that he didn't stop anything, didn't give us any problems."

Stevan Mitchell was among those who valued the chance to get out of the Commission's offices in Rosslyn and into the "real world" of CI. "I think this was…a really very smart thing that General Marsh had placed on our agenda to do…to not just purely be content with the sector representatives that were there around the table with us, but to do some pretty aggressive outreach and to go out and meet with leading representatives of the various infrastructure sectors, talk to them about their security-related concerns and the impediments that they experienced."

Commission members held public meetings in Atlanta, Boston, Houston, Los Angeles, and St. Louis, and attended dozens of conferences and roundtables. Two strategic simulations conducted by Booz Allen Hamilton and Sandia National Laboratory gave members a glimpse of hypothetical crises. To boot, the Commission set up a website to facilitate contact.

By the time the outreach efforts were completed, Commission members had visited with dozens of professional and trade associations, private sector infrastructure users and providers, academia, federal, state and local government agencies, consumers, Congressional Members, their staff, and others. All told, more than 6,000 contacts were made in the course of the Commission's work.

"A lot of freedom was given to these sector teams and to the individual Commissioners to go out and do things," says Jim Kurtz. "Probably some of it was counterproductive. But they went out. They were engaged. They knew who to talk to. They took it on as a mission. They went out and found people."

Bill Harris, DOT's private sector Commissioner, for example, provided personal entrée to the railroad industry where he had longstanding contacts gained during a lifelong career in transportation. Says Tom Falvey, Harris's public sector counterpart, "Bill opened the doors to the industry, so we were able to meet with the senior people within the railroads, the presidents and the CEOs and the operations chiefs…We visited most of the dispatch centers and talked to them about…communication and control systems and what potential vulnerabilities there could be on train systems or on databases that basically ran the business of the railroads."

Thanks to a schedule filled to the brim with such hands-on briefings, the Commission found itself awash in information, particularly anecdotal. "We spent weeks and perhaps even months it seemed in the anecdote phase," notes Marsh. "Everybody was bringing to the Commission all these anecdotes about how bad things could be or were, and examples of what…a new hacker would do…. We finally [had to] say, 'Hey, look, we've got a feel for the problem now. The real important issue is what do we do about it?'"

Lacombe and Kurtz orchestrated the next step, drawing on their experience together at the Commission on Roles and Missions of the Armed Forces (CORM), where they had devised a method informally dubbed the Issue Paper Process. A Commissioner could nominate an issue for discussion by first submitting a two-page paper that the entire group would yea or nay. If the issue was deemed worthy of further discussion, the issue's sponsor would then prepare a longer paper in which he or she laid out things out in more detail and offered options for resolution.

"An issue paper would generally be somewhere between two and ten pages," explains Lacombe. "The paper would explore the issue, define why it's an issue . . . There had to be at least three options for each one. One was a null set option, that is no change. [At the other end] was a radical change unencumbered by political or economic constraints. Then in between were the two or three or maybe only one other option that was explored in terms of pros and cons. That's exactly how they had to present them."

The papers were turned into briefing charts for presentation to the entire group. "Some of the issues went three, four, five days' worth of meetings with no resolution or until you got to a resolution," says Lacombe. "It was a negotiation process."

---

**From *Critical Foundations: Thinking Differently***

During the preparation of the sector papers we identified several dozen issues for which recommendations might be appropriate. Each issue was described, relevant observations, findings, and conclusions were collected, and several alternative recommendations were prepared. The Commission then deliberated each issue and selected one of the alternative recommendations.

---

"Sometimes we spent an afternoon and perhaps didn't get more than two issues discussed," notes Marsh. "But that served a tremendously useful purpose. It brought us together in our thinking. Now, there were obviously some diverse views and they were probably never reconciled."

Mary Culnan, the only full-time university faculty member on the Commission, found the discussion process enlightening for what it

PCCIP Commissioners

revealed about the group's dynamics. "For the military people," says Culnan, "it was, 'Well, the general's in charge, and you just pass [his thoughts] down the chain of command' and that's it. The rest of us… would say what we thought. I think that came as a surprise to some of the military people. I thought, 'Hey, this is just like a faculty meeting. You say what you want.' And I thought that was good."

Culnan also found the Commission "amazingly non-partisan." But non-partisan did not mean un-opinionated. While some Commissioners from the federal establishment tended to be cautious about committing themselves without checking with their home base, the discussions overall were lively, thanks to the varied perspectives brought to the table.

"I don't remember anything that was particularly contentious," says Culnan. "You just had a lot of people in the room, everybody wanted to talk, everybody had a voice, in most cases. I do remember we were running up against a deadline toward the end. Everybody kept pushing to get done."

Marsh notes that the divide between the private sector's and public sector's ways of thinking was ever-present in the discussions. Some agencies felt that they were doing enough in terms of protecting their infrastructure "and didn't need to do a lot more," he notes. "Treasury was especially like that. They felt their systems were totally secure…and consequently, there was no room for further improvement or need for further efforts. I don't think what they grasped was the private sector aspect of it. Yes, you may be doing good work, but what about your private sector counterparts?"

"Some of the agencies, though, grasped the problem," continues Marsh. "DOD obviously grasped the problem right away, understood what it was all about."

Private sector members, too, sometimes brought staunch positions to the table, including the confidently delivered message that industry was on top of the issue, if only because it was in its interest to do so. Industry members also were hesitant to talk bluntly about their vulnerabilities—a hesitancy that the Commission ultimately concluded was one of the chief issues for the private sector and so by extension a big issue for the Commission.

"That's a problem we had with everybody," says Jim Kurtz. "If you talk about your vulnerabilities and you're in the business of providing a service, then as soon as you talk about it, you create liabilities for yourself. You'll either scare business away or something goes wrong and you have now admitted that you're vulnerable and if you didn't do anything about it, you're now liable."

As someone with a bird's eye view of the proceedings, Lacombe identified five distinct and often conflicting perspectives that played into the discussions. Using a computer intrusion as an example, he explains:

"There's a defense perspective, a law enforcement perspective, an intelligence perspective, a civil rights perspective, and a business perspective. That's the way that I thought about it anyway. Whichever perspective you come from, your response to an infrastructure intrusion is different."

"If you're in business, law enforcement comes in and they put the sticky tape around everything, the yellow tape, and they say, 'Stay off your computer system while we do the investigation,'" explains Lacombe. "If you're in business, you don't want that. You want to stop the hurt and get back in business. That's how you stay in business."

"If you're in law enforcement, because your metric of success is successful prosecution which requires identifying the bad guy, which as we know in the cyber area is very hard to do, then you come in and you take over that computer system for however long it takes for you to identify the bad guy."

"If your perspective is DOD—protect the nation—your response is to kill the guy. 'We have offensive information weapon.' Or we assume we do. 'Take one of those and just fry his hard drive or whatever. Just shoot him.'"

"If you're in intelligence, your response is, 'Don't do anything. Let's just listen and learn what we can learn without him knowing that we're here.'"

"And, finally, if you're in the privacy community, your response is, 'Gee, that's too bad, but let's not take any action, read e-mails or anything like that.'"

"We had people representing each of those perspectives and they weren't uncompromising," says Lacombe. "They were very compromising, but those are pretty diverse opinions to try to bring together and none of those interests aren't real. They're all real."

The Commission's formal discussions benefited from the fact that Commissioners could jawbone issues at the office water cooler informally between sessions. The casual exchanges meant that the group wasn't "starting from scratch," says one Commissioner. "You sort of knew everybody's opinion and what research they'd done or what they'd found and kind of what they were thinking.... I think in general it worked fairly well."

As the clock ticked toward deadline, the sprawling research and debate phases began to wind down and the Commission dug into the process of hammering out its conclusions and, ultimately, its recommendations. One of the first products to emerge was a series of five sector reports. Each sector team identified the critical infrastructure in its area, toted up threats and vulnerabilities and proposed solutions. Shorter versions of the reports were later folded into the larger final report.

Although each sector had its own unique characteristics and infrastructure issues, there were inevitably some cross-cutting aspects. SCADA systems, for example, were embedded in more than one sector, notably transportation and energy. Privacy and other legal issues, as already noted, were other areas that had relevance across the board.

In the course of their research, Commissioners began to see other links among sectors. A picture began to emerge that many had not considered before: Infrastructures often intersected with other infrastructures in ways not readily apparent, or taken completely for granted.

Phil Lacombe was among those on the Commission who found the notion of interdependencies an eye-opener: "What the Commission did principally through those infrastructure investigations was it documented the fact that we're, first, dependent on the critical infrastructures and, second, the critical infrastructures are dependent on a cyber background that we didn't understand. We still don't understand it, but then we didn't even know it was there. It was a revelation for some of the Commissioners, as well as for others, that our water systems rely on computer networks and telephone—the ability to use a telephone to dial in to perform maintenance on the water supply system. I didn't think about that stuff before."

---

### From *Critical Foundations: Thinking Differently*

We Found Increasing Dependence on Critical Infrastructures: The development of the computer and its astonishingly rapid improvements have ushered in the Information Age that affects almost all aspects of American commerce and society. Our security, economy, way of life, and perhaps even survival, are now dependent on the interrelated trio of electrical energy, communications, and computers.

System complexities and interdependencies: The energy and communications infrastructures especially are growing in complexity and operating closer to their designed capacity. This creates an increased possibility of cascading effects that begin with a rather minor and routine disturbance and end only after a large regional outage. Because of their technical complexity, some of these dependencies may be unrecognized until a major failure occurs.

---

Bill Joyce, PCCIP Commissioner from the CIA, notes that modern business practices have exacerbated the potential cascading effects of one system breaking down and affecting others in the process. "You assume that a company can accommodate the fact that it loses communications with its customers or suppliers for a certain amount of time, but in fact in just-in-time type of businesses, those downtimes can be critical and cost them a great deal of money and their customer base. So the reliability of the infrastructure is, I think, far more significant than is generally understood in America. We are in a somewhat unusual circumstance if you look at it across the globe."

"We had a specific case we looked at on the Commission," says Bill Harris. "The Lomo Prieto earthquake in California. The gas systems were shut down. Telephone systems were shut down. In both cases, they brought hundreds of people out to help them restore service. Before you can restore gas service, somebody has to be home so that you can check to be sure the pilot light is on before you turn the gas on in the house; otherwise, you create a real hazard, so the gas company started making all kinds of phone calls to find out were people at home. The telephone company saw this spike in phone service. They couldn't stand it, so they cut off their telephone service without any recognition that they were stopping that whole area of restoration service. There'd been no planning, no recognition of the interdependence of these infrastructures. So when we talk about infrastructure interdependence, it isn't just the fact that cyber connects with everything. It's everything else connects with everything."

The "disconnect" between the gas and telephone utilities in the earthquake's aftermath points toward what is perhaps the most important—and most challenging—conclusion of the PCCIP: the importance of information sharing.

In spite of the Commissioners' distinctly varied perspectives, agendas, and levels of technical understanding, "everybody placed information sharing right at the dead center," says Stevan Mitchell.

TIMELINE OF FEDERAL-LEVEL POLICYMAKING: 1997

1997—Operation Eligible Receiver conducted by Department of Defense to analyze vulnerabilities associated with infrastructure dependencies.
1997 October—the PCCIP issues its final report *Critical Foundations: Protecting America's*

*Infrastructures*, characterizing the nation's major infrastructures, defining threats to them and recommending a series of policies for the federal government. The majority of the recommendations were incorporated into PDD 63 in May 1998.

In the process, the group also recognized something else: information sharing was in its way every bit as complex as technological interdependencies. In fact, it was a kind of interdependency of its own, requiring cooperation between two parties—the private sector and the public—that by custom, law, and experience had reasons and rationalizations for dancing warily around one another.

As early Commission discussions had quickly revealed, the private sector felt it had ample cause for hesitating to let government know about problems. Revealing vulnerabilities—much less actual intrusions or problems—seemed to have only downsides. One, of course, was the simple truth that knowledge is power...power, perhaps, to a competitor, a potential regulator, a potential litigant.

As Lacombe pointed out in his example of five attitudes toward how to handle a computer intrusion, the last thing a private sector enterprise wants is a yellow do-not-cross tape encircling its premises and announcing to the world that security has been compromised.

Harris points to the CitiBank episode in 1994 as an example. As soon as the FBI announced that the bank had been attacked successfully by a Russian crime gang, the "bank lost its three best customers the next day. Said CitiBank is not trustworthy. It's that experience that makes all the private sector very concerned about what the FBI is going to do with information that comes from reporting, as good citizens what's happening.... The FBI is interested in convictions, not in the broader problem of CIP."

Lawsuits were another concern brought up by business. "From the standpoint of a company or an industry, if they're going to tell you what their vulnerabilities are, they are creating liabilities for themselves," Jim Kurtz points out. "Because if it becomes known that they knew about those liabilities and didn't do something about them, then they're subject to due diligence kinds of liabilities. That's the whole tension that you work with and I think it's still the fundamental tension."

Stevan Mitchell points to yet another issue: fear of regulation. Companies need to have "confidence that if they were to disclose some of these vulnerabilities to an agency with regulatory authority that that agency wouldn't then turn around and turn it into a rule and basically penalize them for their act of good samaritanship by going to them and saying, 'Look, we've got a problem here, we need to work on it.' Well, they might do better in terms of their bottom line, in terms of preserving the continuity of their own operations, just to keep quiet about it."

In the same vein, many private sector entities are—or at least were—naturally leery of the Freedom of Information Act (FOIA). Mitchell notes that to some degree the fear was ill-founded: "Some companies didn't really understand how the Freedom of Information Act worked and because of that, they didn't understand whether the information that they turned over to a government agency might then have to be made available to the public and to what extent it would be tagged back to them as the contributor." In part because of the efforts of the Commission, the FOIA "impediment," as Mitchell terms it, has diminished substantially thanks to changes in the law pushed by the PCCIP.

Mary Culnan points to a longstanding lack of confidence in the government's handling of information as the basis for distrust. "A lot of organizations had heard about or read about or directly had bad experiences with the federal government or they just felt the risk was too great, so they were not willing to share."

"Basically people have to believe that the risks are manageable and then you go through this kind of loop of experience," continues Culnan. "The trust grows as you have positive experiences and that's not going to happen quickly. That's why it's not a quick fix: people have to disclose a little information, find out that the information is held in confidence, that their trust has not been betrayed. If they were told the information would be used in one way and then it's used in another way, then they're going to say forget it.

"So over time," says Culnan, "if they develop positive experiences with information sharing, then they'll do it and it'll get good word of mouth and other people will get involved. But it's one of those things that is going to take time."

Money, too, is a major factor for the private sector. As Charles Lane pointed out in his 1989 report to the Senate Committee on Government Affairs, the private sector invariably keeps the bottom line—not national security—in sight at all times. Businesses will spend where spending is justified, but only when facts and figures, not rumors, rule the decision.

Culnan recalls hearing the CEO of one of the nation's largest telecommunications companies bluntly state: "'We're spending plenty of money on security. We do this because our business will not survive if we're not secure, and we're not going to spend another nickel unless you can prove to us that there's a need to do so from the government, [so] don't just ask us to do this. You have to tell us. You have to share information with us.'"

"I thought that was a pretty stunning comment," says Culnan. "Sort of summed up what the problem is.... You've got private sector companies that own the infrastructures on which the federal government and everyone depends. The government cannot tell them what to do."

The public sector, on the other hand, has its agenda and obligations, too. Keeping FOIA exemptions as limited as possible was one. The Freedom of Information Act had been put in place to answer public concerns about undue governmental secrecy.

Another issue for government was the question of the public's right to know. David Jones, PCCIP Commissioner from the Department of Energy, points out that at the time of the Commission's deliberations, the Environmental Protection Agency (EPA) was planning to list thousands of hazardous waste sites on a website. "They were going to have all the vulnerabilities of all these 10,000 on one website, so that was quite an issue.... EPA [was] basically saying, 'People have the right to know.'... Of course, if there was a chemical site over here, I ought to have the right to know what's going on...what might happen. Now, that's one thing, but when you put it on one website, then the terrorist, of course...sees everything across the whole country. That upset the Commission and so that was a major issue with EPA."[i]

## EARLY CONCLUSIONS

The issues papers process had given the Commission plenty to think about, and enough to begin drawing some overarching conclusions that would serve as the basis for its recommendations. One of the most important ones was recognizing that the government's own approach to infrastructure protection was not a model.

"We saw that the government wasn't setting the example," says Lacombe. "Government networks were among the most vulnerable in the country. Government's reliance on critical infrastructure was not well understood by the government. At that same time, you had the emergence of the E-government initiatives and the requirements to move into the increasingly paperless electronic relationships between citizens and their government agencies."

"The government of course has to set the standard," says Marsh. "It has to be the benchmark. It needs to get its act together. If it gets its act together, then it's in a position to exhort the private sector to get its act

together. If the government is sitting here as sloppy as it can possibly be—
as it still is, I might add, in my judgment—then how in the world can you
exhort the people out here to fix their systems?"

Another key revelation was the recognition that "when it comes to critical infrastructure protection the national security pyramid is inverted," says
David Keyes. "The pyramid is stood on its head. The federal government is
the least knowledgeable about the inner workings of critical infrastructures,

---

### From *Critical Foundations: Thinking Differently*

A Wide Spectrum of Threats: Of the many people with the necessary
skills and resources, some may have the motivation to cause substantial disruption in services or destruction of the equipment used to provide the service.

This list of the kinds of threats we considered shows the scope of activity with potentially adverse consequences for the infrastructures, and the
diversity of people who might engage in that activity. It may not be possible
to categorize the threat until the perpetrator is identified—for example, we
may not be able to distinguish industrial espionage from national intelligence collection.

Natural events and accidents. Storm-driven wind and water regularly
cause service outages, but the effects are well known, the providers are experienced in dealing with these situations, and the effects are limited in time
and geography.

Accidental physical damage to facilities is known to cause a large fraction of system incidents. Common examples are fires and floods at central
facilities and the ubiquitous back-hoe that unintentionally severs pipes or
cables.

Blunders, errors, and omissions. By most accounts, incompetent,
inquisitive, or unintentional human actions (or omissions) cause a large
fraction of the system incidents that are not explained by natural events and
accidents. Since these usually only affect local areas, service is quickly
restored; but there is potential for a nationally significant event.

Insiders. Normal operation demands that a large number of people
have authorized access to the facilities or to the associated information and
communications systems. If motivated by a perception of unfair treatment

the banking system, electrical power grids, telecommunications networks in an age of convergence. The owners and operators of the business are the best informed, the most knowledgeable and the most capable of dealing with emergencies supported by the private experts and contractors that they get their normal support from. So this inversion of the national security pyramid is one that, in my mind, very much argued against attempting to impose from the unknowledgeable government sector onto the very knowl-

---

by management, or if suborned by an outsider, an insider could use authorized access for unauthorized disruptive purposes.

Recreational hackers. For an unknown number of people, gaining unauthorized electronic access to information and communication systems is a most fascinating and challenging game. Often they deliberately arrange for their activities to be noticed even while hiding their specific identities. While their motivations do not include actual disruption of service, the tools and techniques they perfect among their community are available to those with hostile intent.

Criminal activity. Some are interested in personal financial gain through manipulation of financial or credit accounts or stealing services. In contrast to some hackers, these criminals typically hope their activities will never be noticed, much less attributed to them. Organized crime groups may be interested in direct financial gain, or in covering their activity in other areas.

Industrial espionage. Some firms can find reasons to discover the proprietary activities of their competitors, by open means if possible or by criminal means if necessary. Often these are international activities conducted on a global scale.

Terrorism. A variety of groups around the world would like to influence U.S. policy and are willing to use disruptive tactics if they think that will help.

National intelligence. Most, if not all, nations have at least some interest in discovering what would otherwise be secrets of other nations for a variety of economic, political, or military purposes.

Information warfare. Both physical and cyber attacks on our infrastructures could be part of a broad, orchestrated attempt to disrupt a major U.S. military operation or a significant economic activity.

edgeable and capable private sector what criteria should be put in place. I think the majority of us agreed that the government didn't know enough about what it was doing to be entrusted with legislating that sort of response, rightly or wrongly."

Stevan Mitchell notes that during the course of the Commission's deliberations, his own thinking "shifted away from any sort of regulatory approach to an approach that says, 'How can we help the infrastructures help themselves?'... One of the things that we could help to do through our Commission report was to raise awareness within the infrastructure sector and within government of the nature of the problem. Get them thinking about it, get them invested in it, that all of this would take time. It wasn't going to happen immediately, but I think we were fine with that."

## NEW VULNERABILITIES

In addition to new threats, there were new vulnerabilities as well— many of them, as the Commission saw first-hand in simulations and briefings—delivered courtesy of the cutting-edge technology in which the country excelled.

"The pace of deployment of information technology was such that we could not keep up with it," says Lacombe. "And it all happened without our being aware of what was happening. It doesn't mean there weren't really smart people in academia and elsewhere who were thinking about it, who saw it, who understood it and who tried to raise red flags before. That was certainly the case, but as a nation, as a government, we didn't understand it. We didn't realize that as you pursue the tremendous economic benefits of information systems, you are creating vulnerabilities and dependencies that carried their own seeds of destruction."

In an article in Foreign Policy magazine in 2002, Thomas Homer-Dixon summed up: "Complex terrorism operates like jujitsu—it redirects the energies of our intricate societies against us. Once the basic logic of complex terrorism is understood (and the events of September 11 prove that terrorists are beginning to understand it), we can quickly identify dozens of relatively simple ways to bring modern, high-tech societies to their knees."[ii]

Bill Harris offers a good example. "When we started looking at this back in 1996 at the Commission, the most computer intensive part of transportation was the national airspace system, which the Federal Aviation Administration runs. The air traffic control system was really run on all the computers, legacy systems, [and] software that was developed fifteen years prior. Very few people knew the operating code and really could [not] go in and manipulate it. And it was 'air gapped' from any Internet or any way to access it, so it was pretty foolproof as far as security goes. The big threat on the national airspace system was the next generation system that was being developed at the FAA.... The design of the system was going to be GPS-focused. The administrative systems and the operating systems were going to be linked, so what you had was a possibility of compromise for somebody working on [an] administrative [program], working on the database and that system is actually connecting you to the air traffic control part of it, the operating part of it, which is also connected to the Internet."

---

### From: *Critical Foundations: Thinking Differently*

Classical physical disruptions. A satchel of dynamite or a truckload of fertilizer and diesel fuel have been frequent terrorist tools. The explosion and the damage are so certain to draw attention that these kinds of attacks continue to be among the probable threats to our infrastructures.

New, cyber threats. Today, the right command sent over a network to a power generating station's control computer could be just as effective as a backpack full of explosives, and the perpetrator would be harder to identify and apprehend.

The rapid growth of a computer-literate population ensures that increasing millions of people possess the skills necessary to consider such an attack. The wide adoption of public protocols for system interconnection and the availability of hacker tool libraries make their task easier. While the resources needed to conduct a physical attack have not changed much recently, the resources necessary to conduct a cyber attack are now commonplace. A personal computer and a simple telephone connection to an Internet Service Provider anywhere in the world are enough to cause a great deal of harm.

A would-be terrorist didn't even need access to the Internet, in fact, to wreak major havoc with the GPS.

Says Harris: "We were told that someone could buy some equipment at Radio Shack and cobble it together and totally defeat the GPS near an airport."[iii]

---

[i] In May 2005, the EPA's Super Fund website included a link to a database that allows visitors to look up Super Fund sites by zip code.

[ii] Thomas Homer-Dixon, "The Rise of Complex Terrorism." Foreign Policy (15 January 2002) <http://www.globalpolicy.org/wtc/terrorism/2002/0115complex.htm>.

[iii] At a June 1998 conference on GPS navigation, FAA administrator Langhorne Bond, an advocate of back-ups for the GPS, noted that the PCCIP strongly urged administrators of the GPS navigational system to retain back-up mechanisms to prevent reliance on a single method of navigation.

# CHAPTER 8

# Sticks and Stones to Bits and Bytes:

## The Commission's Recommendations

*"The kindest thing that might be said of American behaviour ten years into the post-Cold War era is that it is astrategic, responding dutifully to the crise du jour with little sense of priority or consistency. A less charitable characterization would be that the United States has its priorities but they are backwards, too often placing immediate intervention in minor conflicts over a 'preventive-defence' strategy focused on basic, long-term threats to security."*

Ashton B. Carter
Survival, Winter 1999/2000 (London)

After devoting countless hours to nailing down the big picture of what could go wrong, the Commission was equally determined to suggest what could, in fact, go right.

Although the Commission itself had the word protection in its name, before the end of its deliberations, there was agreement that a different term was in order—one with more positive connotations. Following a debate that lasted "several days," the group gravitated to the word assurance.

"Many of us with defense backgrounds were familiar with infrastructure security or communication security…protecting, securing the lines of communication," says Phil Lacombe. "Securing the lines of supply has always been important. Now those lines extended into a cyber structure that we couldn't see, couldn't touch, didn't know how to protect...[In fact,] we didn't want to just protect it. What was important about it was that it would be there to operate the way it's supposed to operate. And so the term assurance was settled on. It's become commonly accepted and today, in the cyber world, information assurance is looked at as a discipline almost, and again, for the same reasons."

---

### From: *Critical Foundations: Thinking Differently*:

"It is clear to us that infrastructure assurance must be a high priority for the nation in the Information Age. With escalating dependence on information and telecommunications, our infrastructures no longer enjoy the protection of oceans and military forces. They are vulnerable in new ways. We must protect them in new ways. And that is what we recommend in this report.

The public and private sector share responsibility for infrastructure protection. Our recommendations seek to provide structures for the partnership needed to assure our future security. Further, they seek to define new ways for approaching infrastructure assurance — ways that recognize the new thinking required in the Information Age, the new international security environment emerging from our victory in the Cold War and both the promise and danger of technology moving at breakneck speed.

---

The flipside of infrastructure assurance could be considered infrastructure awareness. During the Commission's outreach phase it had become clear that the average person had little cause to think about infrastructure in more than a passing way. Even then, only if inconvenienced by its breakdown.

"I don't have the stats to back this up," says Stevan Mitchell, "but I would venture to say that more money is probably spent on anti-spam measures than has been spent on personal firewalls [for] PCs. Which just points to the fact that it's the squeaky wheel that gets the grease. It's the thing that's bugging you today that you spend money against and that you take care of, not necessarily the conceivably larger threat that may loom from intrusions and misuse of your computers."

The lack of awareness wasn't surprising. "[T]echnologies are so pervasive as to be 'transparent' to the casual observer," noted Robert Kupperman in 1984, "so much part of civilization as to seem virtually invisible. The extension of technology in the service of civilization has perhaps reached the point of no return, at which the interlocking infrastructure that has evolved is so taken for granted and at the same time so complex as to allow for no realistic alternative."[i]

---

### From *Critical Foundations: Thinking Differently*:

#### Lack of Awareness

We have observed that the general public seems unaware of the extent of the vulnerabilities in the services that we all take for granted, and that within government and among industry decision-makers, awareness is limited. Several have told us that there has not yet been a cause for concern sufficient to demand action. We do acknowledge that this situation seems to be changing for the better. The public news media seem to be carrying relevant articles more frequently; attendance at conferences of security professionals is up; and vendors are actively introducing new security products. The Commission believes that the actions recommended in this report will increase sensitivity to these problems, and reduce our vulnerabilities at all levels.

We Recommend a Broad Program of Awareness and Education: Because of our finding that the public in general and many industry and government leaders are insufficiently aware of the vulnerabilities, we have recommended a broad and continuous program of awareness and education to cover all possible audiences. We include White House conferences, National Academy studies, presentations at industry associations and professional societies, development and promulgation of elementary and secondary curricula, and sponsorship of graduate studies and programs.

---

The sharpest arrow in the Commission's quiver was aimed at the issue that had popped up "dead center" during its research phase: information sharing.

## From *Critical Foundations: Thinking Differently*:

### Infrastructure Protection through Industry Cooperation and Information Sharing

We believe the quickest and most effective way to achieve a much higher level of protection from cyber threats is to raise the level of existing protection through application of best practices. We have accordingly recommended a sector-by-sector cooperation and information sharing strategy. In general, these sector structures should be partnerships among the owners and operators, and appropriate government agencies, which will identify and communicate best practices. We have especially asked the National Institute of Standards and Technology (NIST) and the National Security Agency (NSA) to provide technical skills and expertise required to identify and evaluate vulnerabilities in the associated information networks and control systems. / One very effective practice is a quantitative risk-management process, addressing physical attacks, cyber attacks that could corrupt essential information or deny service, the possibility of cascading effects, and new levels of interdependency. / The first focus of sector cooperation should be to share information and techniques related to risk management assessments. This should include development and deployment of ways to prevent attacks, mitigate damage, quickly recover services, and eventually reconstitute the infrastructure.

We suggest consideration of these immediate actions prior to the completion of a formal risk assessment: (1) Isolate critical control systems from insecure networks by disconnection or adequate firewalls; (2) Adopt best practices for password control and protection, or install more modern authentication mechanisms; (3) Provide for individual accountability through protected action logs or the equivalent.

The sector cooperation and information sharing needed to improve risk assessments and to protect against probable attacks may naturally develop into sharing of information on current status. This would permit assessing whether one of the infrastructures is under a coordinated attack — physical, cyber, or combined. As this process develops, the national center for analysis of such information should be in place and ready to cooperate.

"If we were in a serious national security confrontation," continues Marsh, "what kind of intelligence needs to be made available to the private sector? They're on the front lines out there. They're trying to defend themselves against attack. If they were in a military organization, the intelligence information would go all the way down to the company commander who is subject to attack. Well, isn't there a parallel here with the private sector? They're subject to attack and shouldn't they be a consumer of intelligence just like the company commander or battalion commander is?"

"[Businesses] understand national policy, says Nancy Wong. "What they're begging for, yelling for, screaming for is 'help us understand why it should matter to us.' You've got to translate it into terms that matter to them…not the who. That was a big stopping point. The government said: 'We can't tell you that. We can't tell you who and we can't tell you how we got this information.' Industry never wanted to know that. They can't address the who. They can't address even the when. What they can address is the how and the intentions at times and the what. The what and the how is what they can address….They need to know where to invest…so they can figure out how to defend themselves, but if you don't tell them even that, then they're operating in a vacuum and everything is a threat and everything is a vulnerability."

In 1957, John Redmond of Koppers Company, Inc., had expressed a similar sentiment about the importance of sharing information between the government and industry in the name of industrial preparedness: "I believe it is time for us to look more realistically at this matter of security information. I personally don't think we are taking any degree of risk today in what is released, and I believe that the releasing of information should be advanced to the point where we are actually taking some slight degree of risk in what is released. I don't see how an effective job of planning at any level is going to be possible until that is done."[ii]

## From *Critical Foundations: Thinking Differently:*
### Infrastructure Assurance is a Shared Responsibility

National security requires much more than military strength. Our world position, our ability to influence others, our standard of living, and our own self-image depend on economic prosperity and public confidence. Clear distinctions between foreign and domestic policy no longer serve our interests well. At the same time, the effective operation of our military forces depends more and more on the continuous availability of infrastructures, especially communications and transportation, that are not dedicated to military use. While no nation state is likely to attack our territory or our armed forces, we are inevitably the target of ill-will and hostility from some quarters. Disruption of the services on which our economy and well-being depend could have significant effects, and if repeated frequently could seriously harm public confidence. Because our military and private infrastructures are becoming less and less separate, because the threats are harder to differentiate as from local criminals or foreign powers, and because the techniques of protection, mitigation, and restoration are largely the same, we conclude that responsibility for infrastructure protection and assurance can no longer be delegated on the basis of who the attacker is or where the attack originates. Rather, the responsibility should be shared cooperatively among all of the players.

"I don't think we got polarized too much," says Lacombe, "but there were clearly different fundamental understandings. Which, I think, reflected the larger struggle that the nation was going through....There isn't a fundamental responsibility on either side in which the other has an interest. [The public and private sectors] both have responsibilities; they both have interests.... The responsibility of a banker is to lock his vault, lock his front door, set his alarm switch and walk out. Right? But he's not also charged with protecting his bank from a nuclear missile attack or from a bomb attack or from an attack by a terrorist with a car bomb.... It doesn't mean that they don't suffer if they get one of those attacks, but that these attacks are in the government space. We expect the government to protect us from those things. Well, once you move into the cyber niche, we don't know where to draw those lines.... So then we get to the public/private partnership even more so. We ended up saying it's a shared threat. It's a shared responsibility and there's a shared action that's required."

"What you don't see," says Marsh, "is government in there with a big hammer hammering these people. That was our first inclination. All we got to do is pass a law that says you've got to fix this thing and if you don't, you're going to be penalized.... Heck, this is easy. Well, of course it's not easy and so we debated ad nauseam this question of whose responsibility is it and, of course, we finally concluded it's a shared responsibility but it's principally with the private sector."

Government, on the other hand, was in a position to help by revamping the legal and regulatory structure to catch up with new realities.

---

### From *Critical Foundations: Thinking Differently*:
#### Reconsideration of Laws Related to Infrastructure Protection

Law has failed to keep pace with technology. Some laws capable of promoting assurance are not as clear or effective as they could be. Still others can operate in ways that may be unfriendly to security concerns. Sorting them all out will be a lengthy and massive undertaking, involving efforts at local, state, federal, and international levels. Recognizing the dynamic nature of legal reform, we attempted to lay a foundation through various studies, papers, and a legal authorities database that can aid eventual implementation of our recommendations and assist owners, operators, and government at all levels.

We also offered a number of preliminary legal recommendations intended to jump-start this process of reform. We identified existing laws that could help the government take the lead and serve as a model of standards and practices for the private sector. We identified other areas of law which, with careful attention, can enable infrastructure owners and operators to take precautions proportionate to the threat. We identified still other areas of law that should be molded to enable a greater degree of government-industry partnership in areas such as information sharing.

The concept of overhauling the complex and sometimes conflicting legal and regulatory framework encountered no substantive resistance among Commission members. The Legal Landscapes exercise undertaken by Stevan Mitchell and his team of consultants had amply demonstrated that the law needed to get up to speed.

Less easily resolved was the question of what kind of structure might be warranted to facilitate the information-sharing and partnership aspects that the PCCIP felt were vital to any serious effort to address critical infrastructure.

"We needed to define something that was neither public nor private but both, neither law enforcement nor defense nor business but all three," says Phil Lacombe.

The Commission debated the possibility of recommending creation of an agency to handle all of the functions that seemed to be called for.

---

### From *Critical Foundations: Thinking Differently*:

#### No National Focus

Related to the lack of awareness is the need for a national focus or advocate for infrastructure protection. Following up on our report to the President, we need to build a framework of effective deterrence and prevention. This is not simply the usual study group's lament that no one is in charge. These infrastructures are so varied, and form such a large part of this nation's economic activity, that no one person or oganization can be in charge. We do not need, and probably could not stand, the appointment of a Director of Infrastructures. We do need, and recommend, several more modest ways to create and maintain a national focus on the issues. Protection of our infrastructures will not be accomplished by a big federal project. It will require continuous attention and incremental improvement for the foreseeable future.

#### A National Organization Structure

In order to be effective, recommendations must discuss not only what is to be done, but how it will get done and who will do it. We have recommended the following partnering organizations be established to be responsible for specific parts of our vision:

---

But after assessing the odds of acceptance, the group opted for stopping short of such a dramatic recommendation. Among other things, the Clinton and Gore administration had undertaken a well-publicized "Reinventing Government" initiative that would no doubt have frowned on a proposal to create a major governmental entity. The Clinton-Gore team was trying to cut government, not add to it.

Instead, the Commission settled for recommending structures that Lacombe characterizes as "squishy or soft. Proposing something akin to today's Department of Homeland Security would have been dismissed," says Lacombe.

"We feared that were you to go that far, you would not be taken seriously, he continues. "Now, today, you would. Today, you could make such a recommendation. In fact, we see it already. The Department of Homeland Security is trying to do just that in its infrastructure protection

- *Sector Coordinators* to provide the focus for industry cooperation and information sharing, and to represent the sector in matters of national cooperation and policy;
- *Lead Agencies*, designated within the federal government, to serve as a conduit from the government into each sector and to facilitate the creation of sector coordinators, if needed;
- *National Infrastructure Assurance Council* of industry CEOs. Cabinet Secretaries, and representatives of state and local government to provide policy advice and implementation commitment;
- *Information Sharing and Analysis Center* to begin the step-by-step process of establishing a realistic understanding of what is going on in our infrastructures—of distinguishing actual attacks from coincidental events.
- *Infrastructure Assurance Support Office* to house the bulk of the national staff which is responsible for continuous management and follow-through of our recommendations; and
- *Office of National Infrastructure Assurance* as the top-level policy making office connected closely to the National Security Council and the National Economic Council.

side of the house.[iii] They're talking about partnerships and things like that that six years ago were not possible."

If the Commission was somewhat cautious in its recommendations for structures to carry out the changes it felt were required, it was less so in calling for research and development. Most of the Commissioners supported more exploration and deployment of existing and emerging technologies in detection and identification of intrusions, and delving further into the implications of "interconnected and fully interdependent infrastructures."

Finally, the Commission highlighted at every opportunity its conviction that nothing short of a change in culture—"new thinking"—was called for. People needed to be aware of their dependence on technology, and be conscious as much of its perils as its pleasures. Companies, too, needed to be "thinking differently" about security. The Commission's quiet insistence on the need to change old habits echoed a comment by William E. Haines of the Business and Defense Services Administration, more than forty years earlier, highlighting the novel threat of nuclear attack:

> As we see it, a company plan should include virtually every department of a company and should not be limited to physical security as such. It should not be something written and forgotten. It should be an integral part of the company's day-to-day operations. It should be 'wired in' at the highest management echelon. The threat of atomic attack is a business risk not just another risk which industry management must face.... It seems to us, therefore, that management has a clear and inescapable responsibility to its stockholders, employees and the Nation for getting 'its ducks in a row.'[iv]

"Most of us grew up with 'sticks and stones will break my bones, but words will never hurt me,'" says Phil Lacombe. "Well, words now hurt. The fact is that words translated into bits and bytes could hurt and we had to come to grips with that."

## RACING TO THE FINISH LINE

With the Commission's October deadline fast approaching, Marsh, Lacombe, Kurtz, and their Commission colleagues worked feverishly to put together not only the big final report, but several ancillary in-depth reports. One focused on research and development, and proposed topics that the Commission felt worthy of investigation. Another paper contained the Commission's conclusions and detailed recommendations for how the "national structures" should function. A third lengthy paper titled "Shared Infrastructures: Shared Threats" offered the Commission's analysis of the vulnerabilities and threats facing critical infrastructures. The five sector reports completed earlier in the cycle were also part of the final package to be submitted to the President.

Marsh was adamant about the need to stay on course, in spite of the various delays that had plagued the Commission at its start. "It was a bottomless sump. You could spend a lifetime at this obviously. You could refine or you could dig deeper or you could broaden. But, [we said,] 'We

PCCIP Staff Director Philip Lacombe receives official thanks for his work on the Commission from General Robert T. Marsh, PCCIP Chairman. Lacombe had earlier served as Special Assistant to the Chairman of the Commission on the Roles and Missions of the Armed Forces, a job that prepared him for the challenges of managing the PCCIP's large staff and complex agenda.

think we know what the message here is and we've reached our fundamental conclusions. Let's get them on paper and get them into the system, get a Presidential Directive to implement or direct the implementation and then let the system do the leg work. We're not the implementers. We need to come up with conclusions and findings, recommendations.' You can do that in the time we had and we did it. It was futile to…drag it out forever."

The Commissioners by and large agreed with Marsh's determination to finish, and worked hard to come to consensus on final content and wording.

"Some things we felt strongly about as individuals [were] omitted because the collective wisdom argued against it," says David Keyes. "Despite the territorial beginnings of the individual government

Commissioners, at the end of the day I think everyone acted in the public interest and voted their hearts on what they thought was the right thing to do. Which is not to say that there weren't diverse opinions, but there was respect for the process and you won some and you lost some and that's the way it was."

Says Paul Rodgers, the private sector Commissioner invited by DOE: "One or two commissioners were concerned about the Commission recommending too much money for R&D or too much money for this or that, but nobody went to the point of insisting that their dissent be recorded.... The front of Commission report mentions that not everybody agreed with everything, but nevertheless they came together and settled their differences with a unanimous report."

The group also made a deliberate decision to offer a series of "sixty or seventy different little things," says Stevan Mitchell, rather than a "Top Ten" approach. "We all realized, to a man, that it was inevitable, given the type of cultural change that we were looking to jump start and the unpopularity of any top down regulatory solutions. There was no support for regulatory solutions, either within government or within the private sector. There was no catalyst type event that would cause people to seriously consider the appropriateness of the regulatory or a top down solution. So we realized that the way that we could best influence change was to get a number of these little things going. That's really what led to all of the recommendations that are contained in the Commission's report. And I think it was exactly the right approach to be using at the time."

The Commission went for the "low hanging fruit," says Bill Joyce. "Relatively easy recommendations that you needed to focus on to make initial progress. But we knew that some of the recommendations would be—and are today—still extremely difficult to implement."

One staff member compares the Commission's recommendations to a floor plan: "When you go out and buy a house, you don't have the architect's drawings, which has all the wiring and plumbing and everything else. You get a little bit of floor plan. Well, we [The PCCIP] gave you the floor plan. We didn't give you the architect's drawings. That was very much something that we were aware of."

"When things really got to the nitty gritty and all of us government types just wanted to sit around and jaw on it," says David Keyes, PCCIP Commissioner from the FBI, "General Marsh really cracked the whip and held these long sessions that were definitely violations of the Eighth

Amendment ban on cruel and unusual punishment, demanding resolution of issues and specific language. It was sort of the Bataan Death March there at the end to get the thing done."

Lacombe expresses some ambivalence about reaching the end. On one hand, he thinks that more time would have allowed the Commission to "do the homework required to make recommendations about things like incentives for research and development into cyber protection or other kinds of economic incentives to facilitate increased protection."

On the other hand, there was the danger of diluting "the impact" of the Commission's work. "General Marsh was very adamant about that," says Lacombe. "He wanted it done in as expeditious a fashion as possible. So he pushed us all."

A few things were left on the cutting room floor. An early version of the report was deemed too sensitive and the draft was removed. A compilation of vulnerabilities across all of the sectors also was recognized, says Kurtz, "as very, very sensitive" and likewise was excised from the final package. A few topics were left untouched, too, to the disappointment of a couple of Commissioners. The international aspects of CIP were not included, nor was the topic of tax incentives to "spur industry on," says Marsh.

"We had discussed it at length," he notes, "but we [had] some difficulty in trying to conceptualize how to structure such incentives and where you would cut off between what was their proper responsibility versus what was over and above. I would have liked to have seen a little better representation of that in the Report."

In the end, what the Commission submitted had—to Marsh's way of thinking—a few simple and plainspoken premises: "Essentially, [the recommendations were:] government fix itself, let's get a new partnership here, let's exchange information both ways and let's help the private sector by passing lessons learned and passing threat information, raising the awareness and so on. Let's hope that given good civic responsibility and good understanding of how it affects the bottom line and all of that, the private sector will come around and do its part, and if it doesn't, if there are things that no reasonable corporate leader would make in his shareholders' best interest, if there are things over and above that, then we, the government, need to address those.... We didn't see anything in particular that a prudent businessman shouldn't undertake on his own. That's sort of the bottom line and where we came out."

# Commissioners of the President's Commission on Critical Infrastructure Protection

**Robert T. Marsh, Chairman** — formerly Chairman of Thiokol Corporation

**John R. Powers, Exec. Director** — Federal Emergency Management Agency, Dir. Region V

**Merritt E. Adams** — AT&T, Director, International Switching Unit

**Richard P. Case** — IBM, Director of Technical Strategy Development

**Mary J. Culnan** — Georgetown University, Professor McDonough School of Business

**Peter H. Daly** — Department of the Treasury, Senior Advisor, Office of the Secretary

**John C. Davis** — National Security Agency, Director, National Computer Security Center

**Thomas J. Falvey** — Department of Transportation, National Security Advisor, Office of Intelligence and Security

**Brenton C. Greene** — Department of Defense, Director, Infrastructure Policy Directorate

**William J. Harris** — Texas Transportation Institute, Associate Director

**David A. Jones** — Department of Energy, Director of Policy, Standards and Analysis

**William B. Joyce** — Central Intelligence Agency, Deputy Chief Foreign Broadcast Information Service Engineering Services Group

**David V. Keyes** — Federal Bureau of Investigation

**Stevan D. Mitchell** — Department of Justice, Attorney, Criminal Division's Computer Crime Unit

**Joseph J. Moorcones** — National Security Agency, Asst. Deputy Director for Information Security

**Irwin M. Pikus** — Department of Commerce, Director, Office of Foreign Availability, Bureau of Export Administration

**William Paul Rodgers, Jr.** — National Association of Regulatory Utility Commissioners, Executive Director and General Counsel

**Susan V. Simens** — Federal Bureau of Investigation, Supervisory Special Agent

**Frederick M. Struble** — Federal Reserve Board

**Nancy J. Wong** — Pacific Gas and Electric Company, Manager, Computer and Network Operations

---

Says Kurtz: "I don't know whether we set [the deadline] for ourselves or what, but to produce this thing, we ended up working about three days straight…. It was a small group of people that worked day and night. Mostly staff. Marsh, of course, I guess. Annie Nelson was the one who was standing by, I think, to haul it to the printing plant. Finally hauled it out at three o'clock in the morning to meet whatever the deadline was."

The rush to get the report into print had more to it than mere determination not to extend beyond the extra three months allotted to the

Commission. Marsh, Lacombe and Kurtz were keenly aware that the more hands the report passed through in draft stage, the more the report would be subjected to editing. Marsh wanted the report printed and the Commission disbanded before anyone could begin tinkering with content.

"There was a fear at the end," says Kurtz, "that we would produce this whole report and then instead of being able to have a bunch of copies printed and passed around, our draft report would go into the interagency [process] and they would be free to edit, bowdlerize, cut, extend, whatever."

"We were not getting a whole lot of support [from the White House]," says Nancy Wong, the private sector Commissioner invited by NSA. "Our biggest concern at that time was that whatever the report was, it was going to get changed dramatically at the end if it went through interagency review. But this is a Presidential Commission, [I thought.] It's supposed to be independent. Not supposed to undergo that kind of review and get changed. So we decided to terminate ourselves, which is really abnormal.... Get the report out and close ourselves down. Then it would have to be published [as is] because it's a Presidential document. You send it to a President and then it gets released because that's just the way it works. So it's probably one of the few governmental bodies in history to just shut itself down in order to get things out."

"We wanted the Commission to disband quickly," says Lacombe. "There were probably all kinds of other reasons, but the major reason was so the Report would be the Report and we could not then get word back that 'The Steering Committee wants to change this' and 'These guys want to change that.'... No more discussion."

---

[i] James R. Woolsey and Robert H. Kupperman, America's Hidden Vulnerabilities: Crisis Management in a Society of Networks (Washington: Center for Strategic and International Studies, Georgetown University, October 1984).

[ii] John Redmond, Industry Planning for Continuity of Production (Washington: Industrial College of the Armed Forces, 28 February 1957, Publication No. L57-121) 11.

[iii] The Information Analysis and Infrastructure Protection Directorate at the Department of Homeland Security.

[iv] William E. Haines, Planning for War Production (Washington: Industrial College of the Armed Forces, 27 January 1955, Publication No. L55-89) 8.

# CHAPTER 9

# Critical Foundations:
## The final report of the Commission

*Dear Mr. President:*

*It is a privilege to forward the report of the President's Commission on Critical Infrastructure Protection, Critical Foundations. You asked us to study the critical infrastructures that constitute the life support systems of our nation, determine their vulnerabilities and propose a strategy for protecting them into the future. I believe our report does this."*

General Robert T. Marsh
Chairman, PCCIP
October 13, 1997

S ometime in 1997, before the President's Commission on Critical Infrastructure Protection had finished its work and disbanded, PCCIP Commissioner Brent Greene received a visit from Craig Fields, chairman of the Defense Science Board. Greene recalls that Fields congratulated him heartily on the Commission's effort: "I absolutely applaud what you folks are doing.... What you are doing is groundbreaking."

Naturally, Greene was pleased. Fields, however, wasn't finished: "But I've got some bad news for you. You folks are lap number 1, and it takes three laps before anything like this really takes hold and becomes part of, 'Oh, my God, we need to do something about this!'"

Fields's point was not lost on Greene, who had spent the last several years briefing government officials on infrastructure vulnerabilities, and not always with the degree of success he wanted. In spite of such events as the 1983 Beirut attacks, the 1993 World Trade Center bombing and the 1995 Murrah Federal Building bombing, the prevailing attitude seemed to be, 'It's not going to happen to us. These are just singular events.' Says Greene: "It hadn't gelled as something that we really needed to worry about."

The next "lap"—Lap number 2 of Fields's friendly warning—arrived at midnight on December 31, 1999, when the much-worried-about global rollover of computers to the year 2000 came and went with a whimper, not the dreaded bang. The nearly flawless changeover confounded doomsday predictions and appeared to validate much of the intense government planning that had gone into preparing for the worst.[i]

In the context of critical infrastructure protection, Y2K's value lay in sparking recognition of the interdependence of systems. As the rollover approached, the omnipresence of computers as the underpinning of many basic systems in modern life was no longer just the stuff of fascination for geeks. "It also got people thinking about the problem early enough," says Greene. "[They] were afraid of the Y2K issue…. It started making people realize that in some cases, the cyber stuff really was significant."

Twenty months later, on the morning of September 11, 2001, Lap number 3 of Fields's trilogy arrived. The spectacular attacks on the World Trade Center and Pentagon by operatives of the militant Islamic al-Qaeda network[ii] stunned the world and set in motion the largest government reorganization since the National Security Act of 1947: the birth of the Department of Homeland Security on November 25, 2002.[iii]

Even before the smoke cleared and the sirens stopped, parallels to Pearl Harbor were inevitably drawn. And like Pearl Harbor, much of the public outrage and anger focused on the loss of life and the question of how such a catastrophe could possibly have happened.

For at least a few who had served on the President's Commission on Critical Infrastructure Protection, September 11 evoked yet another response. "We did not know how prophetic we were going to be," says Nancy Wong. "That infrastructures would be a huge part of what the attack would be about. Now, it was not cyber; it was physical. But you saw what happened. They [the 9/11 terrorists] used our transportation system, one of our infrastructures, to attack another infrastructure, which was our financial services and by default, because of the way the telecom system was structured, hit our telecom system."

Tom Falvey, who was still with the Office of Security & Intelligence at the Department of Transportation (DOT) when the attacks occurred, notes that "within DOT, when 9/11 hit we were able to immediately call every sector within transportation and put in measures, [telling them to] 'go talk to them about implementing countermeasures, about sharing threats.' If it hadn't been for the Commission and PDD 63, that organization would never have existed. We wouldn't have known where to start."

Wong's and Falvey's observations are interesting. But the intersection between the PCCIP and the events of September 11 is perhaps less about the prescience or impact of the Commission on the aftermath of the attacks, than about the impact of September 11 on the legacy of the PCCIP.

In the days following the attacks, as the Bush administration and Congress rushed to respond, the Gilmore and Hart-Rudman Commissions[iv] received far more attention than the PCCIP. The lack of media play wasn't surprising. Both commissions were nearer in time to the events. The Gilmore Commission had been established by DOD in 1999 to assess domestic response capabilities for terrorism involving weapons of mass destruction (WMD). One of its recommendations had been the creation of an office in the executive branch dedicated to combating terrorism. The other commission, formally known as the United States Commission on National Security/21st Century, had also issued recommendations, in a February 2001 report titled *Seeking a National Strategy*. Chaired by Senators Gary Hart (D) and Warren Rudman (R), the so-called Hart-Rudman Commission had spoken anxiously of the inevitability of a major terrorist act on U.S. soil, cautioning that "Americans will likely die on American soil, possibly in large numbers" within 25 years, and had recommended the creation of a National Homeland Security Agency.[v]

The PCCIP, on the other hand, had intentionally steered clear of making either such a dire prediction or recommending such a dramatic overhaul in the federal government, having stuck its finger into the political winds of 1997 and gauging that neither fit the tenor of the times.

Reception of the PCCIP's report in October 1997 had, in fact, been pretty flat, at least in the minds of several members of the Commission and its staff. Mary Culnan recalls, "I used to make the joke [that if] we were to get our picture taken with the President, we'd have to go down to the White House and get one of those big cardboard cut-outs [to] pose with him."

President Bill Clinton highlighted the PCCIP's work in a speech given at the U.S. Naval Academy in Annapolis (MD) on May 22, 1998.

"We were invited once to a larger meeting where the President was a hundred feet away from us," says Bill Harris. "That's as close as we ever got. We never were invited to the White House. We could've been the Commission of the Janitor.... I didn't feel that anybody at the White House really cared about what we were doing."

Irv Pikus, a Commissioner who stayed on to run one of the main national structures recommended in *Critical Foundations*, the Critical Infrastructure Assurance Office (CIAO)[vi], was more philosophical: "You can always expect more, but you know, Presidents typically just don't get involved in stuff. They have their own things to do. They set up these commissions and they really don't pay much attention to them. For example, when the shuttle crashed [in 1986], there was a presidential commission on that.[vii] The president really didn't get involved.... The fact that this report [i.e. Critical Foundations] resulted in a Presidential Decision Directive so quickly I think is an indication that they were tuned in. They were waiting for this to happen.... I can't remember a commission effort that got as far as this has so quickly. I think it's rather extraordinary and I think it's largely, or to some extent, due to the fact that people like Sandy Berger [National Security Advisor] and Clinton himself were interested in this."

Tom Marsh, the PCCIP's chairman, was nonetheless disappointed in the low-key public reception accorded the Commission's findings: "I wanted people to speak out publicly on behalf of the product and say they endorsed it. Of course, I wanted the President to say that in the worst way and we got...a short line in one of his speeches over at Annapolis about the [Commission]. But it was very short and that's the only public utterance out of the White House ever on the Commission.[viii] You would think after eighteen months full-time effort to come up with something, and...a PDD that embraced every bit of the conclusions and recommendations...it would warrant also some strong statements out of the bully pulpit. But it didn't."

Efforts to brief Clinton or Gore on the Commission's recommendations proved unsuccessful. Says Phil Lacombe: "I don't think that it was understood by [VP Gore's] senior advisory team enough. Either they were afraid that it would be not popular or they were afraid that it wasn't what [it purported to be], that it wasn't really a national level issue. Plus, of course, they'd already claimed that Gore had invented the Internet and they got clobbered for that. [M]aybe there was a certain amount of gun shyness there. I don't know, but it really was unfortunate that it couldn't get more traction. Sandy Berger, the National Security Advisor, understood it and its importance. Dick Clarke clearly did and he was very senior in that process as well. The Attorney General understood it. The Defense Department understood, but wasn't interested."

The Commission's work did get a nod from a National Defense Panel that had been working at the same time. When the Panel issued its report in 1997,[ix] it explicitly endorsed and urged support for the PCCIP's recommendations:

> As the threats to commercial and defense information networks increase, the defense of our information infrastructure becomes crucial. The Department of Defense's reliance on the global commercial telecommunications infrastructure further complicates the equation. Our response to information warfare threats to the United States may present the greatest challenge in preparing for the security environment of 2010–2020.... The recommendations of the President's Commission on Critical Infrastructure Protection (PCCIP) should be the foundation of our future information security program.

The Panel's brief endorsement pointed to the heart of the Commission's profile problem: *"The threat is diffuse and difficult to identify. Consensus on how to guard against it is difficult to establish."*

The subject of the Commission's work was simply, in the words of Commission consultant Lee Zeichner, "a political loser... a lose-lose, no matter how you look at this issue." First, the term 'critical infrastructure' seemed tailor-made to evoke yawns. Next, like earlier 'duck and cover' campaigns of the 1950s and 1960s, there was always the danger of overplaying the potential for disaster and being derided as a Chicken Little. Finally, if something did happen, human nature would see to it that those who had taken on the issue originally got blamed for whatever went wrong—whether or not such blame was deserved.

Some didn't even wait until anything went awry to criticize. An official response from the EPIC, the Electronic Privacy Information Center, to *Critical Foundations* blasted the Commission for allegedly playing fast and loose with privacy issues.

> The PCCIP proposes the development of a large-scale monitoring strategy for communications networks. Borrowing techniques that have been applied to hostile governments and foreign agents, the PCCIP brings the Cold War home with an open-ended proposal to conduct ongoing surveillance on the communications of American citizens.[x]

The charge confounded PCCIP Commissioner Mary Culnan, who had worked alongside EPIC and other privacy advocates to hash out a "working solution that tried to balance the competing objectives of not putting the information out on the Internet that could be used to blow things up.... [The solution was that] before [groups] decided to put information up on their website, they should do a risk assessment and make a judgment based on the results of the risk assessment. Everybody in the room finally agreed that would be fine, as I recall. Then when the recommendation came out, EPIC just blasted it even though they had been there and agreed."

A presentation at the Ninth Annual Strategy Conference at the U.S. Army War College, held in March 1998, likewise took the Commission to task, calling it "at once a small sign of hope and a large symbol of despair" and suggesting that it had "no doubt...marched to its secret drummer and gave its masters exactly what they wanted—unfortunately, it did not give the nation what it *needed*."[xi] Among other things, the presenter charged the Commission with not having talked to "any of the serious professionals outside the Beltway"—an odd point given the PCCIP's outreach program.

Industry, too, says Nancy Wong, "pushed back on the Commission's reports because they were afraid regulation was coming out and that we were trying to make jobs for everybody, especially since many of the Commissioners were public agency reps.... They thought government was looking for something to do because the Cold War was over and they needed to invent something to spend their time on and money on."

Inside the halls of government, *Critical Foundations* was being reviewed with the kind of turf-oriented eye that had prompted the Commission to hustle to publish its report and put itself out of business. One Commission staff member who stayed on after the report was issued attended interagency meetings "where all the departments got together and had nothing but turf wars and we got nowhere fast. Justice had its ox to gore and Commerce had theirs and Treasury had theirs and had that report not been issued, [it] would not read anywhere [the way] it does today had the Committee had an opportunity to go through it and modify it."

Fifty years earlier, at the time of creation of the National Security Council, Arthur M. Hill, chairman of the National Security Resources Board, noted with humor:

> It is a lesson in patience, in determination, the overcoming of daily frustration in trying to set up a new organization within this government, and particularly one that might be said to impinge on many other departments and agencies of the government.... [O]ne very fundamental fact that has to be realized and that is, that nothing can be accomplished in this democratic government of ours that will be enduring and that will be accepted in a case of emergency unless the thing is chewed up one side and down the other and everyone has a chance to have his say. After that is done and people are pretty well exhausted with their objections, then there is the opportunity to gain acceptance, and it must have acceptance, particularly anything so important as a mobilization…in the stresses and strains of wartime.[xii]

Marsh's perception of the interagency process was more positive: "The only input [from the agencies] as such was when we finally circulated the draft for agency comment. The drafts were very well accepted. Not much change at all and consequently, that says to me, the Commissioners did a good job of prepping their agencies and keeping them abreast of where we were coming out and so on. I really did expect quite a hullabaloo, I guess I would say, when we issued our report because it asked the agencies to do some things that they'd never done before, like facilitate these exchange efforts with the private sector and so forth, but we didn't get any push back on that at all, so I was quite surprised."

On May 22, 1998, Clinton unveiled two Presidential Decision Directives as official follow-ons to the PCCIP's work: PDD 62, "Combating Terrorism" and PDD 63, "Protecting America's Critical Infrastructures."

Clinton briefly described them both during a speech that same day given to the graduating class at the Naval Academy in Annapolis—the speech alluded to by Marsh. Clinton noted "that as we approach the twenty-first century, our foes have extended the fields of battle—from physical space to cyberspace.... Rather than invading our beaches or launching bombers, these adversaries may attempt cyber attacks against our critical military systems and our economic base.... [If] our children are to grow up safe and free, we must approach these new twenty-first century threats with the same rigor and determination that we applied to the toughest security challenges of this century."

Of the two Directives, PDD 62 was perhaps the less complex in content. Most of it was classified, so only a small portion was made public. Among other things, the Directive affirmed that the FBI would continue as the Lead Federal Agency for "crisis management" and the Federal Emergency Management Agency (FEMA) would remain the Lead Federal Agency for "consequence management."

# Presidential Decision Directive 62

May 22, 1998

*Protection Against Unconventional Threats
to the Homeland and Americans Overseas*

## 1. General
It is increasingly likely that terrorist groups, or individuals with criminal intent, may use unconventional methods to disrupt the Nation's critical infrastructure or use weapons of mass destruction (WMD) against our citizens.

As these types of threats mature, it is necessary to prepare to deter them, prevent them from occurring, or, if need be, limit the damage to a minimum. Success is dependent upon possessing the capability for an integrated response, and in the case of critical infrastructure protection, having public/private partnerships.

## 2. Present Achievements and Current Challenges
**Present Achievements:**
- An increased rate of apprehensions and convictions;
- An increase in counterterrorism legislative authorities;
- An increase in the funding for consequence management planning;
- An increase in the importance of terrorism on the diplomatic agenda;
- Growth of assistance to, and cooperation with, other democracies in combating terrorism; and
- Improving and expanding a professionally trained interagency cadre.

**Current Challenges:**
- Terrorist groups may choose asymmetrical attacks on our domestic and international vulnerabilities, through the use of WMD and/or cyber warfare;
- Terrorist groups possess the knowledge, skills, and abilities to use WMD;
- Former "cold war" civil defense programs have been downsized or dismantled, and cities are not prepared to deal with a large-scale event;
- Improvements in technology will make it difficult for law enforcement agencies to detect and prevent terrorist acts; and

- The Nation's critical infrastructure relies heavily on the use of computers, which are prone to cyber attacks.

## 3. Consequences Management

In the event of a terrorism incident, the Federal Government will respond rapidly, working with State and local governments, to restore order and deliver emergency assistance. FEMA, the Lead Federal Agency for consequence management, is responsible for preparing for and responding to the consequences of a WMD incident with participation of other departments and agencies including the Public Health Service (PHS), Environmental Protection Agency (EPA), and Department of Energy (DOE), as necessary. The Department of Justice (DOJ), through the FBI, is the Lead Federal Agency for crisis management and operational response to a weapon of mass destruction incident.

Domestically, key Federal agencies and Departments, through interagency efforts, will continue training and providing equipment to first responders to prepare them for response to WMD incidents. Emphasis will be placed on preparing those responders in the largest 120 cities.

The Department of Defense, in coordination with other Federal Departments and agencies, will provide training to metropolitan first responders and will maintain trained military units to assist State and local responders. One example is the National Guard concept of initially forming 10 Rapid Assessment and Initial Detection (RAID) teams in each FEMA Region. These teams are designed to provide rapid response to a WMD incident and assist State and local responders.

PHS, in the Department of Health and Human Services, is the Lead Federal Agency in planning and preparing for response to WMD-related medical emergencies. PHS will continue supporting State and local governments in developing Metropolitan Medical Strike Teams; maintaining the National Disaster Medical System; and, in conjunction with the Department of Veterans Affairs, stockpiling antidotes and pharmaceuticals in the event of a WMD incident.

## 4. Equipment

DOJ, in coordination with FEMA, will provide equipment to State and local emergency responders.

## 5. Critical Infrastructure

It is imperative that the United States be adequately prepared to deal with attacks on critical infrastructure and cyber systems. As such, the President reviewed the recommendations of the Presidential Commission on Critical Infrastructure Protection and has signed PDD 63, entitled Protecting America's Critical Infrastructures (PDD 63 is For Official Use Only). A white paper, entitled "The Clinton Administration's Policy on Critical Infrastructure Protection: Presidential Decision Directive/NSC-63," is available at www.whitehouse.gov/WH/EOP/NSC/htm/NSCSDoo3.html. This white paper outlines the Administration's program to deal with threats to our Nation's critical infrastructure.

PDD 62 essentially classified, codified and clarified the roles and missions of various agencies engaged in counter-terrorism activities and established a new entity, the Office of the National Coordinator, to integrate and coordinate these activities.

In a move that probably surprised few, Clinton designated Richard Clarke, then the Special Assistant to the President for Global Affairs, National Security Council, to fill the role of National Coordinator. Clarke had been involved in writing the two Presidential Decision Directives.

PDD 63, "Protecting America's Critical Infrastructures," was the more complicated of the two Directives, its main thrust devoted to the creation of the national structures envisioned by the PCCIP. (See Appendix D for a fact sheet covering highlights of the public portion of PDD 63.)[xiii]

The overarching national goal, according to the Directive, was to achieve adequate protection of the nation's critical infrastructure from intentional attacks (both physical and cyber) by the year 2003. Interruptions to critical infrastructure were to be "brief, infrequent, manageable, geographically isolated, and minimally detrimental to the welfare of the United States."

The universe of critical infrastructures to be protected echoed the earlier CIWG and PCCIP exercises in identifying sectors: information and communications; banking and finance; water supply; aviation, highways, mass transit, pipelines, rail, and waterborne commerce; emergency and law enforcement services; emergency, fire, and continuity of government services; public health services; electric power, oil and gas production, and storage.

The Directive also identified four activities where the federal government traditionally controls critical infrastructure:

- internal security and federal law enforcement
- foreign intelligence
- foreign affairs
- national defense

A lead agency was assigned to each of these "sectors." In turn, each lead agency was expected to appoint a **Sector Liaison Official** to interact with private sector organizations. The private sector was encouraged to choose a **Sector Coordinator** to work with the agency's sector liaison official. Together, the liaison official, sector coordinator, and anyone else deemed relevant, were to contribute to a sectoral security plan, which was to be integrated into a **National Infrastructure Assurance Plan**.

Each of the activities normally undertaken primarily by the federal government also was assigned a lead agency, which in turn was to appoint

## Lead Agencies

| DEPARTMENT OR AGENCY | SECTOR OR FUNCTION |
|---|---|
| Commerce | Information and Communications |
| Treasury | Banking and Finance |
| EPA | Water |
| Transportation | Transportation |
| Justice | Emergency Law Enforcement |
| Federal Emergency Management Agency | Emergency Fire Service |
| Health and Human Services | Emergency Medicine |
| Energy | Electric Power, Gas, and Oil |
| Justice | Law Enforcement and International Security |
| Director of Central Intelligence | Intelligence |
| State | Foreign Affairs |
| Defense | National Defense |

a **Functional Coordinator** to coordinate efforts similar to those made by the Sector Liaisons.

PDD 63 also outlined the role that Richard Clarke would play as **National Coordinator** for Security, Infrastructure Protection, and Counterterrorism. The National Coordinator was to report to the President through the Assistant to the President for National Security Affairs.

Among the many duties outlined in PDD 63, the National Coordinator was to hold the chairmanship of the **Critical Infrastructure Coordination Group**, the main interagency working group for developing and implementing policy and for coordinating the federal government's own internal security measures. The CICG included high-level representatives from the lead agencies (including the Sector Liaisons), the National Economic Council, and other relevant agencies.

Each federal agency was made responsible for securing its own critical infrastructure, under the guidance of a **Critical Infrastructure Assurance Officer**—or CIAO. An agency's Chief Information Officer (CIO) could wear both hats. In cases where the CIO and the CIAO weren't the same person, the CIO had responsibility for assuring the agency's information assets (databases, software, computers), while the CIAO would oversee any other assets that fell under the category of critical infrastructure. Agencies were given six months from the signing of the Directive to develop their plans and two years to implement them. Updates were to occur biennially.

Those provisions theoretically took care of CI issues inside the government's own halls, a reflection of the PCCIP's admonition that the federal government needed to get its own act together, instead of being "as sloppy as it can possibly be"—Marsh's frank assessment.

Implementation of this ambition turned out to be one of the more difficult aspects of the Directive's program. The process got off to a rocky start, in part because agencies balked at the reporting requirements or were confused about their obligations.[xiv]

Next, the Directive set about establishing mechanisms designed to kick up cooperation between the public and private sectors. The National Infrastructure Assurance Council (NIAC) was to include private operators of infrastructure assets as well as officials from state and local government, plus a smattering of relevant federal agencies. The Council was charged with meeting periodically and providing reports to the President "as appropriate." Together with his other 'hats,' the National Coordinator was to wear that of Executive Director of the Council.

The Directive also called for a **National Infrastructure Assurance Plan**. The plan was to integrate all of the plans from each of the sectors (mentioned earlier) and could incorporate a vulnerability assessment, including the minimum essential capability required of the sector's infrastructure to meet its purpose; remedial plans to reduce a particular sector's vulnerability; warning requirements and procedures; response strategies; reconstitution of services; education and awareness programs; research and development needs; intelligence strategies; opportunities for international cooperation; and legislative and budgetary requirements.

The ambition was not a small one. To help the National Coordinator pull together all sector plans into a national roadmap, PDD 63 established a National Plan Coordination Staff. The original set-up morphed into an entity called the **Critical Infrastructure Assurance Office** (or CIAO, not to be confused with the agencies' Critical Infrastructure Assurance Officers). The CIAO was housed in the Department of Commerce's Export Administration, a move that consternated some and was later criticized as a poor choice.

The CIAO's plate would be a full one. Among other things, the office was to support the National Coordinator's efforts to integrate the sector plans into a National Plan—no small task—as well as lend a hand to individual agencies in developing their internal plans, help coordinate national education and awareness programs, and provide legislative and public affairs support where necessary.

PDD 63 set as a goal the development of a national capability to detect and respond to cyber attacks while in progress. Without mentioning it specifically in the Directive, the Clinton administration proposed establishing a **Federal Intrusion Detection Network (FIDNET)** that would meet the goal in coordination with the **Federal Computer Intrusion Response Capability (FedCIRC)**[xv], established just before PDD 63's debut.

A few months before PDD 63 was unveiled, the FBI had hustled to set up an entity called the National Infrastructure Protection Center (NIPC), partly in response to a series of attacks on DOD computers during the winter of 1998—an incident dubbed Solar Sunrise. The Directive gave its post facto blessing to the NIPC and called for it to be the focal point for federal threat assessment, early warning, capability, vulnerability analysis, law enforcement investigations, and response coordination. All agencies were required to pass along to the NIPC information about threats and actual attacks on their infrastructure, as well as any attacks on private sector infrastructures that came to their attention.

The FIDNET and FedCIRC were to feed into the NIPC. According to the Directive, the already-established NIPC was to be linked electronically to the rest of the federal government and use warning and response expertise located throughout the federal government. The Directive also made the NIPC the conduit for information sharing with the private sector through an equivalent **Information Sharing and Analysis Center (ISAC)** operated by the private sector, which PDD 63 encouraged the private sector to establish.

The structure and processes laid out in PDD 63 were nothing if not ambitious, at least in terms of nudging existing agencies and programs to "think differently" about infrastructure and security. Whether or not the ambitions could be implemented successfully was another question.

---

[i] Note that the Y2K apparatus was disassembled soon after the rollover, consternating those who felt it was an excellent model for monitoring cyber-based infrastructure attacks. For the official wrap-up of the federal government's Y2K experience, see The Journey to Y2K: Final Report of the President's Council on Year 2000 Conversion (Washington: GPO, 19 March, 2000).

[ii] On September 11, 2001, attacks were carried out by nineteen people affiliated with the al-Qaeda network, a militant Islamic group. The members hijacked four commercial aircraft. Two crashed into the two tallest towers of the World Trace Center in Manhattan. A third aircraft struck the Pentagon outside of Washington, D.C. The fourth crashed into a field near Shanksville (PA), following a passenger rebellion. The death toll of the attack exceeded 2,986, more than the approximately 2400 fatalities experienced at Pearl Harbor on December 7, 1941.

[iii] As of June 2005, the Department of Homeland Security's website was http://www.dhs.gov/dhspublic/. The huge department was organized into four directorates, including Border and Transportation Security, Emergency Preparedness and Response, Science and Technology, and Information Analysis and Infrastructure Protection.

[iv] The federally-chartered "Gilmore Commission" was created in 1999 as the Advisory Panel to Assess Domestic Response Capabilities for Terrorism Involving Weapons of Mass Destruction. The RAND Corporation provided staff support to the commission. The 17-member Gilmore Commission disbanded in early 2004 after issuing its final report. The "Hart-Rudman Commission," created in 1998 as the U.S. Commission on National Security/21st Century, recommended in February 2001 the creation of a new

"Homeland Security Agency." The panel sketched out a major reorganization of the Pentagon, State Department, National Security Council and other agencies. The report also urged Congress to streamline its own committee structure to keep interference in national security matters at a minimum.

ᵛ From the "Hart-Rudman Commission" report, Roadmap for National Security: "We therefore recommend the creation of a new independent National Homeland Security Agency (NHSA) with responsibility for planning, coordinating, and integrating various U.S. government activities involved in homeland security. NHSA would be built upon the Federal Emergency Management Agency, with the three organizations currently on the front line of border security-the Coast Guard, the Customs Service, and the Border Patrol- transferred to it. NHSA would not only protect American lives, but also assume responsibility for overseeing the protection of the nation's critical infrastructure.... Through the commission's proposal for a National Homeland Security Agency, the U.S. government will be able to improve the planning and coordination of federal support to state and local agencies, to rationalize the allocation of resources, to enhance readiness in order to prevent attacks, and to facilitate recovery if prevention fails.... Most important, this proposal [places] the problem of homeland security within the broader framework of U.S. national security strategy.... We are mindful that erecting the operational side of this strategy will take time." (U.S. Commission on National Security/21st Century, Roadmap for National Security, January 2001.)

ᵛⁱ Based at the Department of Commerce.

ᵛⁱⁱ The Presidential Commission on the Space Shuttle Challenger Accident was established by Executive Order 12546, signed February 3, 1986. The accident took place on January 28, 1986, less than one week earlier.

ᵛⁱⁱⁱ President William J. Clinton. Speech to graduating class of U.S. Naval Academy. 22 May 1998.

ⁱˣ National Defense Panel, Transforming Defense: National Security in the 21st Century (Washington: Department of Defense, December 1997).

ˣ Electronic Privacy Information Center, Critical Infrastructure Protection and the Endangerment of Civil Liberties: An Assessment of the President's Commission on Critical Infrastructure Protection (Washington: EPIC, 1998) iii.

ˣⁱ Robert David Steele, "Takedown: Targets, Tools and Technocracy," paper for the Ninth Annual Strategy Conference at the U.S. Army War College, March 1998 <www.fas.org/irp/eprint/takedown1.htm>.

ˣⁱⁱ Arthur M. Hill, National Security Resources Board (Washington: National War College, 6 June 1948) 2.

ˣⁱⁱⁱ Highlights of Presidential Decision Directive 63 are included here. For the White House's white paper on PDD 63, see Appendix D.

ˣⁱᵛ For more background, see John D. Moteff, Critical Infrastructure: Background, Policy, and Implementation (Washington: Congressional Research Service, 17 February 2005, Order Code RL30153.)

ˣᵛ FedCIRC was renamed the Federal Computer Incident Response Center and was later absorbed into the Department of Homeland Security's National Cyber Security Division. FIDNET became a subject of controversy from the start, involving issues of cost, privacy and technical feasibility. By 1998, FIDNET's role as a distributed intrusion detection system feeding into a centralized analysis and warning capability was abandoned.

# CHAPTER 10

# The Real Heart of the Problem:

## Implementation

*"The most urgent need is to establish clearly within the Federal Government the central point of authority and the form of organization which is to plan for and execute the nonmilitary defense of the United States. As I see it, the most important thing today in this area is to come to grasp with the real heart of the problem and to establish a central point of organization to which everyone can look for answers...."*

John H. Redmond
Koppers Company, Inc.
1957

The White House formally issued PDD 62 and PDD 63, but much of the drafting had been done by the PCCIP's "Transition Office," with substantial input from Richard Clarke. The drive to disband the Commission as soon as *Critical Foundations* was issued had not meant that everyone who had served on the PCCIP disappeared back into their previous lives. The Executive Order that extended the Commission's deadline for three months also provided for a few members of the Commission and staff to continue on to support the review process.

Phil Lacombe got the Transition Office up and moving, and then David Keyes took over. Others from the PCCIP who helped with the drafting or other aspects of moving the Commission's work through official channels included Bob Giovagnoni, John Davis, Bill Harris, Bill

Secretary of Homeland Security, Tom Ridge, listens to a reporter's question at his first press conference.

Joyce, Nancy Wong, Paul Rodgers, John Powers, and Lee Zeichner, who had handled much of the Legal Landscapes undertaking at the behest of Stevan Mitchell.

Reaction of Commission members to the contents of the final Directive ran the gamut from satisfied to disappointed.

Bill Harris was among those who felt something had gotten lost in the translation: "PDD 63 doesn't say anything about how important infrastructures are, how crucial they are, the things that they do. It just says the government's going to do this, the government's going to do that. We're going to appoint this guy to do that, that guy to do that…. It doesn't make a case for action and the action that it proposes is just appointing people to posts."

Bill Joyce counters by pointing out that President Decision Directives aren't aimed at the private sector. "[*Critical Foundations* and PDD 63] had two different purposes. One is essentially inspirational and the other one is directive, and the verbiage and the content are completely different. The PDD is much more akin to the Emancipation Proclamation, whereas what the Commission did is much more like the Gettysburg Address. You wouldn't expect a PDD to drive home the case for action. But I don't myself have a position as to what may have been lost or compromised."

## FINDING A HOME FOR CIAO

One of the outcomes of the PDD that gave little satisfaction to a number of Commissioners was the placement of the Critical Infrastructure Assurance Office (CIAO) in the Department of Commerce. "It was…kind of hung on Commerce on grounds that Commerce was the most likely organization to relate to industry," says Bill Harris, "and therefore to the partnership processes that we were hoping to espouse."

Another Commissioner notes that Commerce probably didn't have "a clue what it was getting, but business-wise, that's where it looked like it fit the best."

Commerce, in fact, had played a similar role after World War II, as one of the lead agencies for putting together the industrial mobilization apparatus as part of the general campaign for preparedness. The Business and Defense Services Administration had worked with industry on the development of a wide array of initiatives aimed at fostering continuity of industry in the event of nuclear attack. BDSA had also played liaison to several industry sectors who sat down in the early 1950s with Commerce's encouragement to draw up industry-wide plans.

One of the drawbacks of the decision to put the CIAO in Commerce, in Jamie Gorelick's view, was timing. The placement in Commerce came on the heels of the "whole encryption debate where…the government got crosswise with the technology community by insisting on a very prescriptive approach to encryption…both proscriptive and prescriptive. I think the people in the Commerce Department, in particular, were worried that the government would look too controlling and scare everybody if we were standing up some governmental structure to protect the national infrastructure."

The CIAO was too timid in Gorelick's view. She continues: "We would have been well better off to have a much simpler system in which we paid for an office and a capacity for each industry which would have provided 24x7 warning, a mechanism for sharing of information, a safe haven for the sharing of information outside of anti-trust concerns and privacy concerns and have provided a convening authority for representatives from industry."

One who wasn't disappointed in the Directive was Tom Marsh. He coordinated on the draft directly with Richard Clarke and "didn't see anything getting lost" in the process. "I reviewed it, so if I'd had any major problem, I would have raised it. I obviously emphasized some wording changes that I thought would have emphasized the Information Sharing and Analysis Centers [ISACs]."

## MIXED REVIEWS: THE ISACS

The free-form development of the ISACs following the release of PDD 63 was another source of frustration to some Commissioners. PDD 63 envisioned a single ISAC to serve as the private sector counterpart to the FBI's National Infrastructure Protection Center (NIPC), collecting and sharing

---

**TIMELINE OF FEDERAL-LEVEL POLICYMAKING: 1998 – present**

**1998 February**—creation of the National Infrastructure Protection Center (NIPC) at the FBI, in response to a concentrated series of attacks on computers at the Department of Defense (an incident dubbed "Solar Sunrise.")
**1998 February**—Executive Order 13073 is signed by

President Clinton creating the President's Y2K Conversion Council chaired by John Koskinen. The Council is to ensure a successful millennial turnover for all federal agencies, and to cooperate with state and local governments and the private sector to address the Y2K problem.

incident and response information among its members and facilitating information exchange between the private sector and government. As one analysis of the NIPC pointed out, "It is one of the critical recommendations made [by] the PCCIP and probably one of the hardest to realize."[i]

The idea took off in an unanticipated direction. The original concept of a single ISAC soon evolved into each sector having its own center. Although it took almost two years for the first ISAC to become operational—one in Banking and Finance—soon ISAC's of all types and arrangements began to appear, not all of them officially sanctioned. Their models and missions also took varied forms. Some focused mainly on cyber; others incorporated physical security, too. Some ISACs organized through existing entities like NERC, while other groups contracted out their ISAC development and operations to security firms.

In addition to individual sectors setting up or contemplating ISACs, a number of sectors joined together in late 1999 to form a Partnership for Critical Infrastructure Security to share information and strategies and to identify interdependencies across industry lines. The CIAO acted as a liaison.

"The CIAO was going to let a thousand flowers bloom and let industry come together on its own," says Gorelick. "[But] it's an act against nature for a company to sit down with its competitors and share its vulnerabilities and to share information which is going to give its competitors competitive advantages. It's just not going to happen or if it does happen, it's going to happen on the very slow pace that we have seen. I mean, if you had told me in 1997 that in 2004 we would be where we are today I would've said that's impossible and inadequate. And I think that's largely due to the decision that was made at the end of the Commission's life and that has been carried forward by both the Clinton and Bush administrations, to be extremely hands off. What you hear about the capacities of these ISACs or whatever they're called is just baloney. It's just not true. They do not have substantial capacity."

"I understand why it came out the way it did," says Gorelick, "but I felt that it [CIAO] was too deferential to industry at a time when I didn't think that industry was asking for that deference and that the deference was coming from the government thinking that the deference was appropriate."

Another PDD concept that was slow to become a reality was the National Infrastructure Assurance Council. It took the Clinton administration until July 1999 to formally establish the group. And the President only forwarded the names of nominees just before leaving office.[ii]

## THE ISSUE WITHOUT END: INTERAGENCY TURF

Irv Pikus notes that the "The way the PDD emerged I think was not bad. I think the PDD set forth things pretty well. They reflected most of the important recommendations of the Commission. It changed them a little bit. Someone might say distorted them. Some might say it made them more incremental and I think that's probably the attitude. It became more practical in its implementation through the PDD. Of course, there were certain realities of government attitudes and agency attitudes it reflected at that point. So I think the PDD as it was written was pretty good. How it was implemented, not so good."

One of Pikus's criticisms is the emphasis on cyber in the various programs. The Commission itself had started out with a strong cyber focus, but Pikus notes that "while the early drafts of our report focused pretty heavily on cyber security, I think we got a better balance…although it's still heavily cyber. [W]e got a better balance in the later drafts, but that balance was lost, I think, on Dick Clarke. The Directive was written correctly. I think that was done pretty well, but the way Clarke implemented it, he focused mostly on cyber stuff and I think that was a mistake."

Pikus also notes that the "White House, at least implicitly, had the responsibility for coordinating this whole activity…. [But] this was the most discombobulated activity you could imagine. We had every agency going off on its own direction, nobody putting it together. We had no coordination meetings to speak off. Clarke only wanted to meet with people at the assistant secretary level or above, but those guys were not interested in this stuff…. He didn't want to meet with us and so we were off on our own and when it came time to go to Congress to get budgets, the White House was nowhere to be seen…. When it came time to coordinate the presentations on the Hill and to look for White House support for the committee hearings, it wasn't there. [S]o when we went for our budget, the reaction we got from both the House and the Senate was, 'What the hell is this all about? We don't know anything about the critical infrastructure protection. That should be something that the FBI does.'… So the White House completely dropped the ball on that."

Matters were probably not helped by the release of a GAO report one month before PDD 62 and PDD 63 debuted that declared that the government was spending more money than ever on terrorism, without "any assurance of whether it is focused on the right programs or in the right amounts."[iii]

As it turned out, the Office of Management and Budget (OMB)—which had not been one of the ten agencies represented on the Commission—ended up exercising perhaps the most influence over the fate of PDD 63's intentions. Simply put, OMB held the purse strings. Frank Raines, OMB's Director at the time, had served on the Commission's Principals Committee, but the agency had otherwise had no role.

David Jones recalls his effort to secure OMB's blessing for DOE's critical infrastructure assurance plans, called for under PDD 63: "I can remember sitting across the table from OMB…briefing [them.] And one of the OMB people basically reaching into his pocket and throwing out some change at me and saying, 'That's all you're going to get, Dave.' It was brutal."

Jim Kurtz points to traditional "turf issues" as one of the main reasons that people like Jones failed to get the funding they needed—the perennial theme of not enough toys in the sandbox to satisfy everyone.

"Who has governmental responsibility for information assurance, I think, is one of the issues," he says. "People tend to approach things not from the standpoint of what's right, but what's right for my organization. That's just the way bureaucracies are and, again, that's why you throw something into a commission. You're trying to take people that have all these different points of view and give them a common mission to come up with an answer that all can live with."

"OMB was not represented on the Commission," continues Kurtz. "I don't know why. I don't know what any of the politics were behind that. But I think it was considerable."

The lack of OMB's participation, says Phil Lacombe, "constrained the Commission Report's ability to be adopted and implemented by the White House. It failed to recognize that a very important constituency was

**TIMELINE OF FEDERAL-LEVEL POLICYMAKING: 1996**

**1998 May**—Presidential Decision Directives (PDD) 62 and 63 released by the White House. PDD 62 created the position of National Coordinator for Counterterrorism, Infrastructure Protection and Security under the National Security Council. PDD 63 offered the first comprehensive national policy on critical infrastructure protection and created a framework for future CIP policy decisions.

not included early enough in the process to feel a full sense of ownership over the report. I was never given a piece of paper or anything that said this is what happened, but what I think happened is that the NSC was given the lead for the charter...and were not interested in bringing OMB to it.... OMB was viewed perhaps a little too much as a budgetary organization, as opposed to the larger management role, that they didn't understand the real value of OMB Circular A130, which establishes requirements for protecting computer systems within the government.... I'm sure there was lots of political jockeying."

The leaders of OMB at the time were also a hard sell, notes both Lacombe and Marsh. "We had a little opposition over there," Marsh says diplomatically, explaining that he had the impression that the Commission's existence had not been viewed favorably by some within OMB who felt that its cyber agenda conflicted with OMB's own role as steward of the government's information systems.

Says Jones: "Dick Clarke really wanted all of us to go out there and work with private industry and set up these ISACs and, in fact, he had basically promised to get money through OMB to various departments to help make this happen, but the funds never materialized. That was a critical element post-Commission: the lack of funding through the various departments. Everybody had the same problem—just couldn't get the funding."

## A MIXED LEGACY

In the end, much of what PDD 63 set in motion was absorbed into the fabric of the Department of Homeland Security when the huge department was organized in 2002. How the national structures and other recommendations that the Commission made in *Critical Foundations: Protecting America's Infrastructure* might have fared on their own—espe-

**TIMELINE OF FEDERAL-LEVEL POLICYMAKING:** 1998 – present

**1998 August**—creation of the National Commission on Terrorism by Congress in response to two bombings of U.S. embassies in Africa. The Commission was led by L. Paul Bremer, a former State Department Ambassador-at-large for counterterror-

ism. It June 2000 report called for stronger controls over international students and recommended the military, not FEMA or the FBI, act as first responder to any terrorist attack on U.S. soil.

cially in light of OMB's apparent lack of support—is, of course, impossible to know.

Many of the Commissioners—at least those interviewed for this book—voice disappointment and worry about the pace and scale of implementation of things they consider urgent priorities: among them, information sharing, awareness, partnership. "I think the strength of what he [Marsh] and the staff did, was in preparing the really rich factual background that showed our vulnerabilities and also what could be done to address them," says Jamie Gorelick. "I think the failure was in the structure that emanated from it. I didn't agree with the very light governmental touch vis a vis industry (e.g. the CIAO, ISACs)."

"I think it's apparent that the private sector hasn't done nearly as much as we had hoped it would do by this time," says Marsh. "In other words, PDD 63 says today that we should be essentially protected against a debilitating attack on the infrastructure.[iv] Well, we're not, so…. I think it's time to re-raise the question and seriously address whether or not we need to incentivize or require increased protective measures to be taken on the part of the private sector. Now, incidentally, not only the private sector but the government sector as well, but that's another matter. So I would take another look at it. I go back to all of our deliberations where we said, 'Well, we ought to at least try and do everything within our power to let the free market economy get this job done.' There were some bitter discussions on that whole matter. Finally the position came out, as I think it should: 'Let's expect the private sector to do that.' Well, the private sector hasn't and so is it now time to readdress that question and see whether or not we need to put in place some regulatory requirements, whether we need to put in place some tax incentives or other financial incentives in order to spur investment in this area."

**TIMELINE OF FEDERAL-LEVEL POLICYMAKING: 1998 – present**

**1998**—creation of the **Critical Infrastructure Assurance Office** (CIAO) as called for by PDD 63. CIAO, located in the Department of Commerce, had responsibility for coordinating the development of critical infrastructure sector plans by the private sector and their respective federal agency liaisons. Drawing on the content of the sector plans, CIAO was then to assist in producing the **National Infrastructure Plan**.

Commissioners also tend to be torn about whether more attention needs to be accorded to threats or to vulnerabilities.

"I think the Commission Report would have been stronger if it had highlighted vulnerability issues and spent less time on threats," says Dave Jones. "Even subsequent to our work, Dick Clarke finally came to that realization that focusing on threats was a waste of time. You really have to focus on the vulnerabilities. [Donald Rumsfeld or] it may have been someone else [said] that if you focus only on vulnerabilities, you'll [spend] yourself to death.... You can identify vulnerabilities. You can do something about them. Threats are much more difficult."

Bill Harris urges the opposite: "Unless you've got a better fix on the threats that we currently have I don't see how we're going to be able to deal with the prevention problem.... It may be that all of our speculation and my speculation about areas that are vulnerable don't make any sense. Terrorists wouldn't think of using his assets up on trying to blow up a bridge when in fact he can blow up a building with the same amount of energy and a building can maybe kill a couple of thousand of people [but with] a bridge, he just delays service. So, I don't have a fix myself yet on how to think about what a terrorist is thinking about. I can only speculate that if he's going to be worried about attacking Yankee Stadium or attacking the Super Bowl, I just don't know."

Some also worry that the events of September 11 will shift attention too much away from cyber issues and leave the nation vulnerable to a catastrophic attack that will not merely cripple infrastructure but undermine the economy and public confidence.

"The government's dramatic, appropriate and effective response to 9/11," says Stevan Mitchell, "I think gives the average person a false sense of complacency that the government's also going to do this with respect to

TIMELINE OF FEDERAL-LEVEL POLICYMAKING: 1998 – present

1999 April—DOD Secretary William Cohen named Virginia Governor James Gilmore to head a blue-ribbon commission "to assess domestic response capabilities for terrorism involving weapons of mass destruction (WMD)." In the first of four annual reports to Congress, the Gilmore Commission declared that the possibility that terrorists will use "weapons of mass destruction (WMD) in this country to kill and injure Americans, including those responsible for protecting and saving lives, presents a genuine threat to the United States."

our cyber vulnerabilities. And that's precisely the opposite of what needs to happen. What needs to happen…is for people and companies to assume more personal responsibility, not less, and to the extent that 9/11 may be highlighting the effectiveness of government-centric solutions, I think it's pointing us in precisely the wrong direction."

Not everyone, however, agrees with the level of urgency that marked much of the Commission's work. A December 2002 Center for Strategic and International Studies (CSIS) report on the risk of cyberterrorism downplayed some of the fundamental fears that are often recited as reasons for taking pre-emptive action against an "electronic Pearl Harbor"[v]:

> A preliminary review…suggests that computer network vulnerabilities are an increasingly serious business problem but that their threat to national security is overstated. Modern industrial societies are more robust than they appear at first glance. Critical infrastructures, especially in large market economies, are more distributed, diverse, redundant and self-healing than a cursory assessment may suggest, rendering them less vulnerable to attack. In all cases, cyber attacks are less effective and less disruptive than physical attacks. Their only advantage is that they are cheaper and easier to carry out than a physical attack.… Cyber-terrorists would need to attack multiple targets simultaneously for long periods of time to create terror, achieve strategic goals or to have any noticeable effect. For most of the critical infrastructure, multiple sustained attacks are not a feasible scenario for hackers, terrorist groups or nation states (particularly for nation states, where the risk of discovery of what would be universally seen as an act of war far outweigh the limited advantages gained from cyber attacks on infrastructure.[vi]

There were also outstanding issues that the Commission didn't—or couldn't—address in the timeframe in which its work needed to be completed. For example, the persuasive role that the auditing and insurance communities could play in holding businesses to high security standards. Or the ticklish dilemma of outsourcing software development and control systems overseas to countries that might or might not share the U.S.'s priorities.

"I can understand why the government was clueless when the tipping point was reached of the transition of control of critical infrastructures from humans to automated systems," says David Keyes. "There is in my mind no excuse for the government to be oblivious to the national security and national economic security considerations of off-shoring the very capabilities upon which the control of those automated networks depend."

In spite of concerns about work left to be done, Commissioners who served on the PCCIP also point to a number of things that they believe the Commission contributed that might otherwise not have happened. For example, trying to jumpstart more R&D in areas related to critical infrastructure assurance. Recognizing that the problem isn't one that either the private or public sector can solve alone. Clarifying or resolving—or even just discussing—some of the privacy concerns that often stand in the way of private sector cooperation with the government. Helping to raise public awareness of the issues.

"I think the Commission helped to raise awareness," says Jim Kurtz. "Public awareness.... Private awareness.... Maybe both. The Commission certainly caused the government to pay attention to its own problem."

"I'm amazed at how much of this has been implemented, absolutely amazed," says Nancy Wong. "And in the timeframe, because I was told by outsiders at the time that [*Critical Foundations*] would be a paper document sitting on a shelf. And I went, 'Well, you know what, at least it's there. Okay?' And you can't say that [now]. I came to Washington to get this document done. But you can't say that it didn't get done and the alerts didn't come out.... What surprised the heck out of me was that this thing within six months had a Presidential Decision Directive behind it."

"So often, studies by big commissions often end up recommending more study," says Kurtz. "The President's Commission recommended something that led to PDD 63."

## REINVENTING GOVERNMENT...AGAIN

In the end the Commission's work was perhaps less about protecting critical infrastructure than it was about reinventing government.

"Part of what PCCIP did was recommend a new governance framework," says Lee Zeichner, a consultant to the Commission. "At the end of the day, if you said tell me one thing they did, they recommended a new governance framework for all the disparate things.... They picked and chose the different philosophies and then the big recommendation was,

'This is a national security issue.' What's the definition of critical infrastructures? Those essential services for which if they are debilitated would cause national economic, national security or public health and welfare crises. That's the National Security Council.... PDD 63 created a new governance mechanism which plucked out pieces of each of those old conventional legacy philosophies and then set [the mechanism] in motion."

"My feeling today is the Commission probably went out too far on some of its assertions with regard to problems," says Joyce, "but not as far as some of the recommendations that were discussed. We pulled back in some areas.... I won't go too far, and say we almost recommended something like Department of Homeland Security, but we pulled back on that knowing that the opposition would be so—.... I think the sense was it would be such a dramatic recommendation that it would destroy any other recommendation that we made, but we definitely were thinking in terms of, 'This is 1947 all over again, that this is a time to re-look at how government is structured. Is it properly structured to deal with the new kinds of threats versus what we've dealt with for 50 years?'"

Indeed, according to *Critical Foundations*, the group recognized early in its deliberations that "the federal government was still organized along Cold War lines. The structure in place had proven very effective at focusing federal attention and resources and on physical threats posed by military, terrorist or criminal entities. Likewise, the relationship between government agencies and infrastructure operators were appropriate to the environment. Except for down-sizing, the structure had not changed significantly since the Cold War, and its relationships with infrastructure owners and operators—though less regulatory in nature—had not changed markedly."[vii]

TIMELINE OF FEDERAL-LEVEL POLICYMAKING: **1998 — present**

**1998 October**—inaugural meeting of the U.S. Commission on National Security in the 21st Century. The Commission was known as the Hart-Rudman Commission for its co-chairmen, Senators Gary Hart (D) and Warren Rudman (R). The Commission reported three times, in 1999, 2000 and 2001. Among other things, the Commission recommended creation of a homeland security organization modeled on the Federal Emergency Management Agency (FEMA).

"Whenever you have a project," notes Joyce, "if that's the focus of your project, it's easy to magnify its significance, but it really has to be put in the context of what came before it, what was going on at the time and what came after it, which doesn't necessarily mean the results or the direct results. I think the Commission was a step, an important step. I'd have difficulty singling it out from a number of other activities as being any more significant or even less significant than other activities. This was a continuum that goes back at least to this Report and beyond."

The continuum that Joyce mentions could be said to extend back in time to the very beginnings of the Republic, when the tiny federal government began to wrestle with its Constitutional duty to provide for the "common defense." For more than a century, the methods of warfare remained relatively stable and so did the responses. But as the nation grew in political stature and military strength, the rules of the game changed. By 1950 and the beginning of the Cold War, it looked like the rules might stay in place indefinitely—or at least until one side or the other pulled the fatal trigger.

When the Cold War ended, it was time to rethink the rules. But government doesn't change on a dime. And neither do mindsets or attitudes. Even when the PCCIP issued its report—together with recommendations geared to the political sensibilities of the times—there were disbelievers and detractors on hand to dismiss its conclusions.

"You had different constituencies who didn't think that the Commission should have arrived at the place that it arrived at," says Phil Lacombe. "I think by and large everyone was surprised by the type of report you got out of the Commission and after people read it and understood it, there's a lot less surprise that it's endured over time. It's interesting in that regard. It really has held up and I think it's because the

**TIMELINE OF FEDERAL-LEVEL POLICYMAKING: 1998 – present**

**2000 January**—the White House released the National Plan for Information Systems Protection Version 1.0: An Invitation to Dialogue, the culmination of two years of work by the CIAO.
**2001 October**—Creation of the Office of Homeland Security, headed by Tom Ridge.

**2002 November**—Elevation of the Office of Homeland Security to Cabinet status as the Department of Homeland Security. More than 170,000 federal employees from two dozen agencies were brought together under one umbrella. CIAO was one of the agencies absorbed into DHS.

From *Industry Planning for Continuity of Production,*
a speech given by John H. Redmond, an Assistant Vice President
of Koppers Company, Inc. in February 1957 to students at the
Industrial College of the Armed Forces.

"*Are there any signs pointing towards a solution to the vulnerability of industry to atomic or thermonuclear attack?*

*I believe that what we can say is this: We are not in a position where we can say there will be no damage and no disruption of production. We haven't progressed to the point where we can keep the enemy completely away from dropping some bombs on the targets and getting some sabotage effectively accomplished.*

*However, I think we can say that some planning is being done. Progress has been made, and that progress has been made is reducing the probable hurt to industry and increasing our ability to mount and support the offensive.*

*I would not want to leave any impression that I believe the job is done or that we are even on the threshold of success. As I have indicated, there is much to do in the sprawling organizations of the National, State and local governments to establish one clear point of responsibility and authority for industrial defense planning and to prepare government for the job of maintaining order and effective government in the postattack period. There is need for more information to be made available to industry and to the general public so that they may better realize the real and serious nature of the threat with which we are living.... We need to recognize that there is a necessity and a compulsion for us to do something now about all phases of both military and nonmilitary defense if we are to survive.*

*I am reminded a little bit of the story of the young couple who were going to hospital to have their first baby. As the nervous prospective father was helping his very anxious wife into the emergency room of the hospital he turned to her and said, 'Dear, are you sure you want to go through with this?' I think that's about where we stand.*"

Commission did exercise restraint.... A lot of what the Commission Report does is explain what's going on and help you come to grips with that fundamental thing that had to change. How to think about it. But it didn't give a lot of concrete recommendations about how to do it."

In the end, the legacy of the Commission could well turn out to be both subtle and powerful...and extremely challenging to assess:

"I think a lot of people significantly underplay how significant the results of the Commission were and how much it changed people's thinking," says PCCIP Commissioner Brent Greene. "It got people thinking in a different direction. Whether you remembered it as being a President's Commission or whether it was critical infrastructure or not, people were thinking about things in a different way because of the Commission. But it was still only a first lap."

"The job of the Commission," says Lacombe, "was to figure out that the world had changed, that fundamental things like what the nation relies on for its security had changed, and we had to help the world see its way clear there."

"This was solving a problem before it became a problem," suggests Tom Falvey. "I used to tell my bosses at DOT: 'If we do our job right, our jobs go away because it [security] becomes part of the procedures, the budgets, the cultures, of an organization that makes security absolutely essential and part of the business practice rather than a cost center.'"... And so I used to tell my boss that if I do my job right, we won't hear about any attacks, we won't hear about breakdowns. The economy will continue to run and security will become part of everyday life and maybe in ten or twenty years, people will say of the Commission, 'It was irrelevant, nothing ever happened.'... I think the things that are happening now on security [are] because of what the Commission did, because the Commission has put the infrastructure in place. The country was able to respond and DHS has been organized. It would not have been able to respond the way it did if the Commission and PDD 63 hadn't at least started the framework to have government and industry working together."

"Are we better off than we would've been had we not had the Commission?" asks Jamie Gorelick. "Way better. Do the compendia that it produced even yet today one hopes inform the efforts on national infrastructure protection? Yes. One would hope. Did we raise the temperature on these issues? Yes, but Nunn and I...both would just rail to each other about the fact that you couldn't get anyone to pay attention to this. We tried. We gave speeches. We went to talk to editorial boards.... And it's because people don't pay attention to issues that are not front and center. And this won't be front and center until there's some really big problem."

In some ways, the Commission can't be credited too much with breaking new ground—after all, the vulnerabilities and threats they explored weren't entirely brand-new—others had been issuing warnings for years. On the other hand, by getting the threats and the vulnerabilities out on the table and turning them over in a more public context, the Commission perhaps shook things up enough—albeit quietly—to set institutional change in motion.

"I recently attended [2004] a DOD-wide CIP conference," says Bill Joyce. "I was very, very struck by how far the DOD has gone in grappling with these issues. They're being discussed at a much higher level than they were when the Commission was in existence. I was quite impressed by some of the discussions. We all have a long way to go and they have a long way to go, but they've really shown that they're committed to CIP."

"Government is...like a big 3,000 pound steel ballbearing," says Jim Kurtz. "It moves really, really slowly and if you try and stop it, you're going to get crushed. So the best you can try and do is to try and change its direction a little bit; there's an inertia but there's also momentum and so some big thing like [Critical Foundations] will come out and they say, 'You guys didn't solve anything.' No, but you put things in motion. I don't know that [things have] played themselves out right now. [But] people are able to talk about the problem of infrastructure vulnerability in terms that were defined by the PCCIP that they wouldn't have talked about otherwise. I think people can talk about this now in ways they couldn't. There's a slow dawning and awareness and if you can articulate it well, people get the story. And I think we told a pretty good story."

---

i For more background, see John D. Moteff, Critical Infrastructure: Background, Policy, and Implementation (Washington: Congressional Research Service, 17 February 2005, Order Code RL30153.)

[ii] The Clinton Administration released Executive Order 13130 in July, 1999, formally establishing the council. Just prior to leaving office, President Clinton put forward the names of 18 appointees. The Order was rescinded by the Bush Administration before the Council could meet. In Executive Order 13231, President Bush established a National Infrastructure Advisory Council (with the same acronym, NIAC) whose functions were similar to those of the earlier proposed Council. On September 18, 2002, President Bush announced his appointment of 24 people to serve on Council. The Executive Order that amended 13231 made some minor modifications to NIAC. For example, the Council now reports to the President through the Secretary of Homeland Security. (United States, General Accounting Office, Critical Infrastructure Protection: Federal Efforts Require a More Coordinated and Comprehensive Approach for Protecting Information Systems (Washington: GAO, report number GAO-02-474, 15 July 2002).

[iii] United States, General Accounting Office, Combating Terrorism: Threat and Risk Assessments Can Help Prioritize and Target Program Investments (Washington: GAO, Letter Report, GAO/NSIAD-98-74, 9 April 1998) <http://www.access.gpo.gov/cgi-bin/get-doc.cgi?dbname=gao&docid=f:ns98074.txt.>

[iv] The end date for reaching full infrastructure protection was 2003 under the goals set out by PDD 63.

[v] The phrase "electronic Pearl Harbor" appears to have first been used in War and Anti-War: Survival at the Dawn of the 21st Century by Alvin and Heidi Toffler (New York: Little, Brown and Company, 1993: 149).

[vi] James A. Lewis, Assessing the Risks of Cyberterrorism, Cyber War and Other Cyber Threats, Center for Strategic and International Studies, Georgetown University (December 2002).

[vii] President's Commission on Critical Infrastructure Protection, Critical Foundations: Protecting America's Infrastructures (Washington: President's Commission on Critical Infrastructure Protection, October 1997) 48.

# Appendix A
## CIPP Oral History Interview Participants

**Mary Culnan** (C)—Slade Professor Management and Information Technology, *Bentley College*

**Thomas J. Falvey** (C)—Chief, Customer Service Division, *National Communications System (NCS)*

**Jamie Gorelick** (A, W)—Partner, *Wilmer, Cutler, Pickering, Hale and Dorr, LLP*

**Brenton Greene** (C)—Vice President for Strategic Initiatives, *Lucent Technologies, Inc.*

**William Harris** (C)—Vice President of Research, *Association of American Railroads (Ret.)*

**David Jones** (C)—Infrastructure Assurance Consultant, *Argonne National Laboratory*

**William Joyce** (C)—Senior Policy Analyst, *SAIC*

**David Keyes** (C)—Chief Operating Officer, *Policy, Analytical and Security Service, Inc.*

**Jim Kurtz** (S)—Research Staff Member, *Institute for Defense Analyses*

**Phillip Lacombe** (S)—Sr. Vice-President and General Manager, *Integrated Systems and Security Business, SAIC*

**General Robert T. Marsh** (C)—United States Air Force (ret.)

**Stevan Mitchell** (C)—Vice President, Intellectual Property Policy, *Entertainment Software Alliance*

**Joseph Moorcones** (C)—Vice President, Worldwide Information Security, *Johnson & Johnson*

**Irwin Pikus** (C)—Visiting Professor of Systems Engineering, *University of Virginia*; Homeland Security Consultant

**John Powers** (C)—Chairman, *CCRI*

**Paul Rodgers** (C)—Executive Director and General Counsel, *National Association of Regulatory Utility Commissioners (ret.)*

**Michael Vatis** (W)—Fmr. Founder and Director, *National Infrastructure Protection Center (NIPC)*

**Nancy Wong** (C)—Director, Office of Planning and Partnerships, Information Analysis and Infrastructure Protection (IAIP) Directorate, *Department of Homeland Security*

**Lee Zeichner** (PC)—President, *Zeichner Risk Analytics*

---

C  = Commissioner
S  = Senior Staff
A  = Advisory Group Member
W  = CIWG Participant
PC = PCCIP Consultant

# Appendix B

## Executive Staff of the PCCIP

Phillip E. Lacombe, *Staff Director*
James H. Kurtz, COL, USA, *Chief of Staff/Executive Secretary*
Janet B. Abrams, *Director of External Affairs/White House Liaison*
Robert E. Giovagnoni, *Col, USAF, General Counsel*
Adrienne M. Griffen, *Executive Assistant to the Chairman*
Elizabeth (Betsy) Harrison, *Director of Legislative Affairs*
Brian P. Hoey, *Lt Col, USAF, Executive Assistant to the Chairman*
Nelson M. McCouch III, *MAJ, USA, Director of Public Affairs*
Monica Y. McNeil, *Executive Assistant to the Chief of Staff/Assistant
    Executive Secretary*
Annie N. Nelson, *Director of Administration*
Carla L. Sims, *Director of Public Affairs*
Lawrence P. St. Marie, *SMSgt, USAF, Executive Officer*
Sona A. Virdi, *Executive Assistant to the Staff Director*

## Professional Staff

Elizabeth A. Banker
Gary R. Boyd
Patricia E. Burt
Julie Consilvio
Frederick S. Davidson
L. C. J. Jacobson
Gary P. Kosciusko

Lloyd E. Lutz Jr., Lt Col, USAF
Carol M. Medill
T. Lynette Proctor
Pamela D. Saunders
James J. Stekert
Stephen T. York

## Support Staff

Bernard R. Robinson, *Deputy Director of Administration*
Bonnie L. Julia, *SFC, USA, NCOIC*
Karen R. Allen, *SrA, USAF*
Becky Love
Robert W. Boyd, *YN2, USN*
Gerald T. Posey, *TSgt, USAF*
Joseph A. Broadway, *YN1, USN*
Sandra M. Robinson, *SSgt, USAF*
Patrick Barlow
Sandra L. Scroggs
Eric J. Cline
Mike Seabron

James E. Crawford, *SSG, USA*
Sherrie M. Smith, *SGT, USA*
Debra A. Dawson, *SSG, USA*
Sharon S. Strippoli
Roada Dickerson, *SrA, USAF*
Shawn R.L. Vincent, *Sgt, USAF*
Elizabeth S. Ellingboe, *SSgt, USAF*
Scott A. Ward
Jeffrey G. Estep, *SSgt, USAF*
Brian W. Young, *SrA, USAF*
Troy L. Joyner, *SSG, USA*
Ed Young
Peter D. LeNard

## Senior Consultants

William A. Buehring
Ramesh Maraj
Mary F. Dunham
Gabe Maznick
Ron E. Fisher
Willis J. Ozier
Paul W. Hanley
Paul Byron Pattak
Peter Gossens
James P. Peerenboom
Duane G. Harder
George J. Rothstein
Michael T. Hovey
Lee M. Zeichner
Joelle Jordan

## Additional Support:

Ed Appel
Paul H. Richanbach
Frederick L. Frostic
Kathleen Robertson
Bill Garber
Elizabeth Sauer
Seymour Goodman
Paula Scalingi
David Graham
James Schlesinger
Michael Leonard
Suzy Tichenor
Stephen J. Lukasik
Larry Welch

# Appendix C

## President's Commission on Critical Infrastructure Protection

### PRINCIPALS COMMITTEE
- Robert E. Rubin, *Secretary of Treasury*
- William J. Perry, *Secretary of Defense*
- Janet Reno, *Attorney General*
- William M. Daley, *Secretary of Commerce*
- Federico Peña, *Secretary of Transportation*
- Hazel O'Leary, *Secretary of Energy*
- John Deutch, *Director of Central Intelligence*
- Franklin D. Raines, *Director of the Office of Management and Budget*
- James L. Witt, *Director of Federal Emergency Management Agency*
- Samuel R. Berger, *Assistant to the President for National Security Affairs*
- Leon Fuerth, *Assistant to the Vice President for National Security Affairs*
- Gene Sperling, *Assistant to the President for Economic Policy and Director of National Economic Council*
- Dr. John H. Gibbons, *Assistant to the President and Director of the Office of Science and Technology Policy*

### STEERING COMMITTEE
- Robert T. Marsh, *Chairman, PCCIP*
- Janet Reno, *Attorney General*
- John J. Hamre, *Deputy Secretary of Defense*
- Donald Kerrick, *Deputy Assistant to the President for National Security Affairs*
- Don Gips, *Deputy Assistant to the Vice President for National Security Affairs*

## ADVISORY COMMITTEE

- Senator Sam Nunn, *Co-Chair*
- Ms. Jamie Gorelick, *Co-Chair*
- Dr. Jeffrey Jaffe
- Ms. Maurice Greenberg
- Mr. David Campbell
- Mr. Joseph Holmes
- Ms. Margaret Greene
- Mr. Charles Lee
- Mr. Erle Nye
- Mr. Elvin Moon
- Mr. Robert Baxter
- Mr. Floyd Emerson Wick
- Mr. Norm Mineta
- Mr. Mort Topfer
- Mayor Sharon Sayles Belton
- Mr. Jerome Davis
- Dr. Robert Berdahl

# Appendix D

## THE WHITE HOUSE
## WASHINGTON
May 22, 1998

## PRESIDENTIAL DECISION DIRECTIVE/NSC-63

Memorandum for the Vice President
   The Secretary of State
   The Secretary of the Treasury
   The Secretary of Defense
   The Attorney General
   The Secretary of Commerce
   The Secretary of Health and Human Services
   The Secretary of Transportation
   The Secretary of Energy
   The Secretary of Veterans Affairs
   Administrator, Environmental Protection Agency
   The Director, Office of Managment and Budget
   The Director of Central Intelligence
   The Director Federal Emergency Management Agency
   The Assistant to the President for National Security Affairs
   The Assistant to President for Science and Technology
   The Chairman, Joint Chiefs of Staff
   The Director, Federal Bureau of Investigation
   The Director, National Security Agency

## SUBJECT: CRITICAL INFRASTRUCTURE PROTECTION

### I. A Growing Potential Vulnerability

The United States possesses both the world's strongest military and its largest national economy. Those two aspects of our power are mutually reinforcing and dependent. They are also increasingly reliant upon certain critical infrastructures and upon cyber-based information systems.

Critical infrastructures are those physical and cyber-based systems essential to the minimum operations of the economy and government. They include, but are not limited to, telecommunications, energy, banking and finance, transportation, water systems and emergency services, both governmental and private. Many of the nation's critical infrastructures have historically been physically and logically separate systems that had little interdependence. As a result of advances in information technology and the necessity of improved efficiency, however, these infrastructures have become increasingly automated and interlinked. These same advances have created new vulnerabilities to equipment failure, human error, weather and other natural causes, and physical and cyber attacks. Addressing these vulnerabilities will necessarily require flexible, evolutionary approaches that span both the public and private sectors, and protect both domestic and international security.

Because of our military strength, future enemies, whether nations, groups or individuals, may seek to harm us in non- traditional ways including attacks within the United States. Because our economy is increasingly reliant upon interdependent and cyber-supported infrastructures, non-traditional attacks on our infrastructure and information systems may be capable of significantly harming both our military power and our economy.

### II. President's Intent

It has long been the policy of the United States to assure the continuity and viability of critical infrastructures. I intend that the United States will take all necessary measures to swiftly eliminate any significant vulnerability to both physical and cyber attacks on our critical infrastructures, including especially our cyber systems.

### III. A National Goal

No later than the year 2000, the United States shall have achieved an initial operating capability and no later than five years from today the

United States shall have achieved and shall maintain the ability to protect the nation's critical infrastructures from intentional acts that would significantly diminish the abilities of:

- the Federal Government to perform essential national security missions and to ensure the general public health and safety;
- state and local governments to maintain order and to deliver minimum essential public services.
- the private sector to ensure the orderly functioning of the economy and the delivery of essential telecommunications, energy, financial and transportation services.

Any interruptions or manipulations of these critical functions must be brief, infrequent, manageable, geographically isolated and minimally detrimental to the welfare of the United States.

### IV. A Public-Private Partnership to Reduce Vulnerability

Since the targets of attacks on our critical infrastructure would likely include both facilities in the economy and those in the government, the elimination of our potential vulnerability requires a closely coordinated effort of both the government and the private sector. To succeed, this partnership must be genuine, mutual and cooperative. In seeking to meet our national goal to eliminate the vulnerabilities of our critical infrastructure, therefore, we should, to the extent feasible, seek to avoid outcomes that increase government regulation or expand unfunded government mandates to the private sector.

For each of the major sectors of our economy that are vulnerable to infrastructure attack, the Federal Government will appoint from a designated Lead Agency a senior officer of that agency as the Sector Liaison Official to work with the private sector. Sector Liaison Officials, after discussions and coordination with private sector entities of their infrastructure sector, will identify a private sector or counterpart (Sector Coordinator) to represent their sector.

Together these two individuals and the departments and corporations they represent shall contribute to a sectoral National Infrastructure Assurance Plan by:

- assessing the vulnerabilities of the sector to cyber or physical attacks;
- recommending a plan to eliminate significant vulnerabilities;
- proposing a system for identifying and preventing attempted major attacks;

- developing a plan for alerting, containing and rebuffing an attack in progress and then, in coordination with FEMA as appropriate, rapidly reconstituting minimum essential capabilities in the aftermath of an attack.

During the preparation of the sectoral plans, the National Coordinator (see section VI), in conjunction with the Lead Agency Sector Liaison Officials and a representative from the National Economic Council, shall ensure their overall coordination and the integration of the various sectoral plans, with a particular focus on interdependencies.

### V. Guidelines

In addressing this potential vulnerability and the means of eliminating it, I want those involved to be mindful of the following general principles and concerns.

- We shall consult with, and seek input from, the Congress on approaches and programs to meet the objectives set forth in this directive.
- The protection of our critical infrastructures is necessarily a shared responsibility and partnership between owners, operators and the government. Furthermore, the Federal Government shall encourage international cooperation to help manage this increasingly global problem.
- Frequent assessments shall be made of our critical infrastructures' existing reliability, vulnerability and threat environment because, as technology and the nature of the threats to our critical infrastructures will continue to change rapidly, so must our protective measures and responses be robustly adaptive.
- The incentives that the market provides are the first choice for addressing the problem of critical infrastructure protection; regulation will be used only in the face of a material failure of the market to protect the health, safety or well-being of the American people. In such cases, agencies shall identify and assess available alternatives to direct regulation, including providing economic incentives to encourage the desired behavior, providing information upon which choices can be made by the private sector. These incentives, along with other action, shall be designed to help harness the latest technologies, bring about global solutions to international problems, and enable private sector owners and operators to achieve and maintain the maximum feasible security.
- The full authorities, capabilities and resources of the government, including law enforcement, regulation, foreign intelligence and

defense preparedness shall be available, as appropriate, to ensure that critical infrastructure protection is achieved and maintained.

- Care must be taken to respect privacy rights. Consumers and operators must have confidence that information will be handled accurately, confidentially and reliably.
- The Federal Government shall, through its research, development and procurement, encourage the introduction of increasingly capable methods of infrastructure protection.
- The Federal Government shall serve as a model to the private sector on how infrastructure assurance is best achieved and shall, to the extent feasible, distribute the results of its endeavors.
- We must focus on preventive measure as well as threat and crisis management. To that end, private sector owners and operators should be encouraged to provide maximum feasible security for the infrastructures they control and to provide the government necessary information to assist them in that task. In order to engage the private sector fully, it is preferred that participation by owners and operators in a national infrastructure protection system be voluntary.
- Close cooperation and coordination with state and local governments and first responders is essential for a robust and flexible infrastructure protection program. All critical infrastructure protection plans and action shall take into consideration the needs, activities and responsibilities of state and local governments and first responders.

## VI. Structure and Organization

The Federal Government will be organized for the purposes of this endeavor around four components (elaborated in Annex A).

*1. Lead Agencies for Sector Liaison:* For each infrastructure sector that could be a target for significant cyber or physical attack, there will be a single U.S. Government department which will serve as the lead agency for liaison. Secretary rank or higher to be the Sector Liaison Official for that area and to cooperate with the private sector representatives (Sector Coordinators) in addressing problems related to critical infrastructure protection and, in particular, in recommending components of the National Infrastructure Protection Plan. Together, the Lead Agency and the private sector counterparts will develop and implement a Vulnerability Awareness and Education Program for their sector.

*2. Lead Agencies for Special Functions:* There are, in addition, certain functions related to critical infrastructure protection that must be chiefly performed by the Federal Government (national defense, foreign affairs, intelligence, law enforcement). For each of those special functions, there shall be a Lead Agency which will be responsible for coordinating all of the activities of the United States Government in that area. Each lead agency will appoint a senior officer of Assistant Secretary rank or higher to serve as the Functional Coordinator for that function for the Federal Government.

*3. Interagency Coordination:* The Sector Liaison Officials and Functional Coordinators of the Lead Agencies, as well as representatives from other relevant departments and agencies, including the National Economic Council, will meet to coordinate the implementation of this directive under the auspices of a Critical Infrastructure Coordination Group (CICG), chaired by the National Coordinator for Security, Infrastructure Protection and Counter-Terrorism. The National Coordinator will be appointed by me and report to me through the Assistant to the President for National Security Affairs, who shall assure appropriate coordination with the Assistant to the President for Economic Affairs. Agency representatives to the CICG should be at a senior policy level (Assistant Secretary or higher). Where appropriate, the CICG will be assisted by extant policy structures, such as the Security Policy Board, Security Policy Forum and the National Security and Telecommunications and Information System Security Committee.

*4. National Infrastructure Assurance Council:* On the recommendation of the Lead Agencies, the National Economic Council and the National Coordinator, I will appoint a panel of major infrastructure providers and state and local government officials to serve as my National Infrastructure Assurance Council. I will appoint the Chairman. The National Coordinator will serve as the Council's Executive Director. The National Infrastructure Assurance Council will meet periodically to enhance the partnership of the public and private sectors in protecting our critical infrastructures and will provide reports to me as appropriate. Senior Federal Government officials will participate in the meetings of the National Infrastructure Assurance Council as appropriate.

## VII. Protecting Federal Government Critical Infrastructures

Every department and agency of the Federal Government shall be responsible for protecting its own critical infrastructure, especially its cyber-based systems. Every department and agency Chief Information Officer (CIO) shall be responsible for information assurance. Every department and agency shall appoint a Chief Infrastructure Assurance Officer (CIAO) who shall be responsible for the protection of all of the other aspects of that department's critical infrastructure. The CIO may be double-hatted as the CIAO at the discretion of the individual department. These officials shall establish procedures for obtaining expedient and valid authorities to allow vulnerability assessments to be performed on government computer and physical systems. The Department of Justice shall establish legal guidelines for providing for such authorities.

No later than 180 days from the issuance of this directive, every department and agency shall develop a plan for protecting its own critical infrastructure, including but not limited to its cyber-based systems. The National Coordinator shall be responsible for coordinating analyses required by the departments and agencies of inter-governmental dependencies and the mitigation of those dependencies. The Critical infrastructure Coordination Group (CICG) shall sponsor an expert review process for those plans. No later than two years from today, those plans shall have been implemented and shall be updated every two years. In meeting this schedule, the Federal Government shall present a model to the private sector on how best to protect critical infrastructure.

## VIII. Tasks

Within 180 days, the Principals Committee should submit to me a schedule for completion of a National Infrastructure Assurance Plan with milestones for accomplishing the following subordinate and related tasks.

1. *Vulnerability Analyses:* For each sector of the economy and each sector of the government that might be a target of infrastructure attack intended to significantly damage the United States, there shall be an initial vulnerability assessment, followed by periodic updates. As appropriate, these assessments shall also include the determination of the minimum essential infrastructure in each sector.

2. *Remedial Plan:* Based upon the vulnerability assessment, there shall be a recommended remedial plan. The plan shall identify timelines, for implementation, responsibilities and funding.

3. *Warning:* A national center to warn of significant infrastructure attacks will be established immediately (see Annex A). As soon thereafter as possible, we will put in place an enhanced system for detecting and analyzing such attacks, with maximum possible participation of the private sector.

4. *Response:* We shall develop a system for responding to a significant infrastructure attack while it is underway, with the goal of isolating and minimizing damage.

5. *Reconstitution:* For varying levels of successful infrastructure attacks, we shall have a system to reconstitute minimum required capabilities rapidly.

6. *Education and Awareness:* There shall be Vulnerability Awareness and Education Program within both the government and the private sector to sensitize people regarding the importance of security and to train them in security standards, particularly regarding cyber systems.

7. *Research and Development:* Federally-sponsored research and development in support of infrastructure protection shall be coordinated, be subject to multi-year planning, take into account private sector research, and be adequately funded to minimize our vulnerabilities on a rapid but achievable timetable.

8. *Intelligence:* The Intelligence Community shall develop and implement a plan for enhancing collection and analysis of the foreign threat to our national infrastructure, to include but not be limited to the foreign cyber/information warfare threat.

9. *International Cooperation:* There shall be a plan to expand cooperation on critical infrastructure protection with like-minded and friendly nations, international organizations and multinational corporations.

10. *Legislative and Budgetary Requirements:* There shall be an evaluation of the executive branch's legislative authorities and budgetary priorities regarding critical infrastructure, and ameliorative recommendations shall be made to me as necessary. The evaluations and recommendations, if any, shall be coordinated with the Director of OMB.

The CICG shall also review and schedule the taskings listed in Annex B.

## IX. Implementation

In addition to the 180-day report, the National Coordinator, working with the National Economic Council, shall provide an annual report on the implementation of this directive to me and the heads of departments and agencies, through the Assistant to the President for National Security Affairs. The report should include an updated threat assessment, a status report on achieving the milestones identified for the National Plan and additional policy, legislative and budgetary recommendations. The evaluations and recommendations, if any, shall be coordinated with the Director of OMB. In addition, following the establishment of an initial operating capability in the year 2000, the National Coordinator shall conduct a zero-based review.

## Annex A: Structure and Organization

**Lead Agencies:** Clear accountability within the U.S. Government must be designated for specific sectors and functions. The following assignments of responsibility will apply.

*Lead Agencies for Sector Liaison:*

| | |
|---|---|
| Commerce | Information and communications |
| Treasury | Banking and finance |
| EPA | Water supply |
| Transportation | Aviation |
| | Highways (including trucking and intelligent transportation systems) |
| | Mass transit |
| | Pipelines |
| | Rail |
| | Waterborne commerce |
| Justice/FBI | Emergency law enforcement services |
| FEMA | Emergency fire service |
| | Continuity of government services |
| HHS | Public health services, including prevention, surveillance, laboratory services and personal health services |
| Energy | Electric power |
| | Oil and gas production and storage |

*Lead Agencies for Special Functions:*

Justice/FBI ..............Law enforcement and internal security

CIA .........................Foreign intelligence

State.........................Foreign affairs

Defense ...................National defense

In addition, OSTP shall be responsible for coordinating research and development agendas and programs for the government through the National Science and Technology Council. Furthermore, while Commerce is the lead agency for information and communication, the Department of Defense will retain its Executive Agent responsibilities for the National Communications System and support of the President's National Security Telecommunications Advisory Committee.

**National Coordinator:** The National Coordinator for Security, Infrastructure Protection and Counter-Terrorism shall be responsible for coordinating the implementation of this directive. The National Coordinator will report to me through the Assistant to the President for National Security Affairs. The National Coordinator will also participate as a full member of Deputies or Principals Committee meetings when they meet to consider infrastructure issues. Although the National Coordinator will not direct Departments and Agencies, he or she will ensure interagency coordination for policy development and implementation, and will review crisis activities concerning infrastructure events with significant foreign involvement. The National Coordinator will provide advice, in the context of the established annual budget process, regarding agency budgets for critical infrastructure protection. The National Coordinator will chair the Critical Infrastructure Coordination Group (CICG), reporting to the Deputies Committee (or, at the call of its chair, the Principals Committee). The Sector Liaison officials and Special Function Coordinators shall attend the CIGC's meetings. Departments and agencies shall each appoint to the CIGC a senior official (Assistant Secretary level or higher) who will regularly attend its meetings. The National Security Advisor shall appoint a Senior Director for Infrastructure Protection on the NSC staff.

A National Plan Coordination (NPC) staff will be contributed on a non-reimbursable basis by the departments and agencies, consistent with law. The NPC staff will integrate the various sector plans into a National Infrastructure Assurance Plan and coordinate analyses of the U.S.

Government's own dependencies on critical infrastructures. The NPC staff will also help coordinate a national education and awareness program, and legislative and public affairs.

The Defense Department shall continue to serve as Executive Agent for the Commission Transition Office, which will form the basis of the NPC, during the remainder of FY98. Beginning in FY99, the NPC shall be an office of the Commerce Department. The office of Personnel Management shall provide the necessary assistance in facilitating the NPC's operations. The NPC will terminate at the end of FY01, unless extended by Presidential directive.

### Warning and Information Centers

As part of a national warning and information sharing system, I immediately authorize the FBI to expand its current organization to a full scale *National Infrastructure Protection Center (NIPC)*. This organization shall serve as a national critical infrastructure threat assessment, warning, vulnerability, and law enforcement investigation and response entity. During the initial period of six to twelve months, I also direct the National Coordinator and the Sector Liaison Officials, working together with the Sector Coordinators, the Special Function Coordinators and representatives from the National Economic Council, as appropriate, to consult with owners and operators of the critical infrastructures to encourage the creation of a private sector sharing and analysis center, as described below.

*National Infrastructure Protection Center (NIPC):* The NIPC will include FBI, USSS, and other investigators experienced in computer crimes and infrastructure protection, as well as representatives detailed from the Department of Defense, the Intelligence Community and Lead Agencies. It will be linked electronically to the rest of the Federal Government, including other warning and operations centers, as well as any private sector sharing and analysis centers. Its mission will include providing timely warnings of international threats, comprehensive analyses and law enforcement investigation and response.

All executive departments and agencies shall cooperate with the NIPC and provide such assistance, information and advice that the NIPC may request, to the extent permitted by law. All executive departments shall also share with the NIPC information about threats and warning of attacks and about actual attacks on critical government and private sector infrastructures, to the extent permitted by law. The NIP will include elements responsible for warning, analysis, computer investigation, coordinating emergency response, training, outreach and development and application of technical tools. In addition, it will establish its own relations directly with others in the private sector and with any information sharing and analysis entity that the private sector may create, such as the Information Sharing and Analysis Center described below.

The NIPC, in conjunction with the information originating agency, will sanitize law enforcement and intelligence information for inclusion into analyses and reports that it will provide, in appropriate form, to relevant federal, state and local agencies; the relevant owners and operators of critical infrastructures; and to any private sector information sharing and analysis entity. Before disseminating national security or other information that originated from the intelligence community, the NIPC will coordinate fully with the intelligence community through existing procedures. Whether as sanitized or unsanitized reports, the NIPC will issue attack warnings or alerts to increases in threat condition to any private sector information sharing and analysis entity and to the owners and operators. These warnings may also include guidance regarding additional protection measures to be taken by owners and operators. Except in extreme emergencies, the NIPC shall coordinate with the National Coordinator before issuing public warnings of imminent attacks by international terrorists, foreign states or other malevolent foreign powers.

The NIPC will provide a national focal point for gathering information on threats to the infrastructures. Additionally, the NIPC will provide the principal means of facilitating and coordinating the Federal Government's response to an incident, mitigating attacks, investigating threats and monitoring reconstitution efforts. Depending on the nature and level of a foreign threat/attack, protocols established between special function agencies (DOJ/DOD/CIA), and the ultimate decision of the President, the NIPC may be placed in a direct support role to either DOD or the Intelligence Community.

*Information Sharing and Analysis Center (ISAC):* The National Coordinator, working with Sector Coordinators, Sector Liaison Officials and the National Economic Council, shall consult with owners and operators of the critical infrastructures to strongly encourage the creation of a private sector information sharing and analysis center. The actual design and functions of the center and its relation to the NIPC will be determined by the private sector, in consultation with and with assistance from the Federal Government. Within 180 days of this directive, the National Coordinator, with the assistance of the CICG including the National Economic Council, shall identify possible methods of providing federal assistance to facilitate the startup of an ISAC.

Such a center could serve as the mechanism for gathering, analyzing, appropriately sanitizing and disseminating private sector information to both industry and the NIPC. The center could also gather, analyze and disseminate information from the NIPC for further distribution to the private sector. While crucial to a successful government-industry partnership, this mechanism for sharing important information about vulnerabilities, threats, intrusions and anomalies is not to interfere with direct information exchanges between companies and the government.

As ultimately designed by private sector representatives, the ISAC may emulate particular aspects of such institutions as the Centers for Disease Control and Prevention that have proved highly effective, particularly it extensive interchanges with the private and non-federal sectors. Under such a model, the ISAC would possess a large degree of technical focus and expertise and non-regulatory and non-law enforcement missions. It would establish baseline statistics and patterns on the various infrastructures, become a clearinghouse for information within and among the various sectors, and provide a library for historical data to be used by the private sector and, as deemed appropriate by the ISAC, by the government. Critical to the success of such an institution would be its timeliness, accessibility, coordination, flexibility, utility and acceptability.

### Annex B: Additional Taskings

## STUDIES

The National Coordinator shall commission studies on the following subjects:

- Liability issues arising from participation by private sector companies in the information sharing process.
- Existing legal impediments to information sharing, with an eye to proposals to remove these impediments, including through the drafting of model codes in cooperation with the American Legal Institute.
- The necessity of document and information classification and the impact of such classification on useful dissemination, as well as the methods and information systems by which threat and vulnerability

information can be shared securely while avoiding disclosure or unacceptable risk of disclosure to those who will misuse it.

- The improved protection, including secure dissemination and information handling systems, of industry trade secrets and other confidential business data, law enforcement information and evidentiary material, classified national security information, unclassified material disclosing vulnerabilities of privately owned infrastructures and apparently innocuous information that, in the aggregate, it is unwise to disclose.
- The implications of sharing information with foreign entities where such sharing is deemed necessary to the security of United States infrastructures.
- The potential benefit to security standards of mandating, subsidizing, or otherwise assisting in the provision of insurance for selected critical infrastructure providers and requiring insurance tie-ins for foreign critical infrastructure providers hoping to do business with the United States.

## PUBLIC OUTREACH

In order to foster a climate of enhanced public sensitivity to the problem of infrastructure protection, the following actions shall be taken:

- The White House, under the oversight of the National Coordinator, together with the relevant Cabinet agencies shall consider a series of conferences: (1) that will bring together national leaders in the public and private sectors to propose programs to increase the commitment to information security; (2) that convoke academic leaders from engineering, computer science, business and law schools to review the status of education in information security and will identify changes in the curricula and resources necessary to meet the national demand for professionals in this field; (3) on the issues around computer ethics as these relate to the K through 12 and general university populations.
- The National Academy of Science and the National Academy of Engineering shall consider a round table bringing together federal, state and local officials with industry and academic leaders to develop national strategies for enhancing infrastructure security.
- The intelligence community and law enforcement shall expand existing programs for briefing infrastructure owners and operators and senior government officials.

- The National Coordinator shall (1) establish a program for infrastructure assurance simulations involving senior public and private officials, the reports of which might be distributed as part of an awareness campaign; and (2) in coordination with the private sector, launch a continuing national awareness campaign, emphasizing improving infrastructure security.

## INTERNAL FEDERAL GOVERNMENT ACTIONS

In order for the Federal Government to improve its infrastructure security these immediate steps shall be taken:

- The Department of Commerce, the General Services Administration, and the Department of Defense shall assist federal agencies in the implementation of best practices for information assurance within their individual agencies.
- The National Coordinator shall coordinate a review of existing federal, state and local bodies charged with information assurance tasks, and provide recommendations on how these institutions can cooperate most effectively.
- All federal agencies shall make clear designations regarding who may authorize access to their computer systems.
- The Intelligence Community shall elevate and formalize the priority for enhanced collection and analysis of information on the foreign cyber/information warfare threat to our critical infrastructure.
- The Federal Bureau of Investigation, the Secret Service and other appropriate agencies shall: (1) vigorously recruit undergraduate and graduate students with the relevant computer-related technical skills full-time employment as well as for part-time work with regional computer crime squads; and (2) facilitate the hiring and retention of qualified personnel for technical analysis and investigation involving cyber attacks.
- The Department of Transportation, in consultation with the Department of Defense, shall undertake a thorough evaluation of the vulnerability of the national transportation infrastructure that relies on the Global Positioning System. This evaluation shall include sponsoring an independent, integrated assessment of risks to civilian users of GPS-based systems, with a view to basing decisions on the ultimate architecture of the modernized NAS on these evaluations.

- The Federal Aviation Administration shall develop and implement a comprehensive National Airspace System Security Program to protect the modernized NAS from information-based and other disruptions and attacks.
- GSA shall identify large procurements (such as the new Federal Telecommunications System ETS 2000) related to infrastructure assurance, study whether the procurement process reflects the importance of infrastructure protection and propose, if necessary, revisions to the overall procurement process to do so.
- OMB shall direct federal agencies to include assigned infrastructure assurance functions within their Government Performance and Review Act strategic planning and performance measurement framework.
- The NSA, in accordance with its National Manager responsibilities in NSD 42, shall provide assessments encompassing examinations of U.S. Government systems to interception and exploitation; disseminate threat and vulnerability information; establish standards; conduct research and development; and conduct issue security product evaluations.

## ASSISTING THE PRIVATE SECTOR

In order to assist the private sector in achieving and maintaining infrastructure security:

- The National Coordinator and the National Infrastructure Assurance Council shall propose and develop ways to encourage private industry to perform periodic risk assessments of critical processes, including information and telecommunications systems.
- The Department of Commerce and the Department of Defense shall work together, in coordination with the private sector, to offer their expertise to private owners and operators of critical infrastructure to develop security-related best practice standards.
- The Department of Justice and Department of the Treasury shall sponsor a comprehensive study compiling demographics of computer crime, comparing state approaches to computer crime and developing ways to deterring and responding to computer crime by juveniles.

[signature]
Bill Clinton

# Critical Infrastructure Protection Program

The Critical Infrastructure Protection (CIP) Program is Congressionally sponsored and uniquely situated at the George Mason University (GMU) School of Law in Arlington, Virginia. Built upon a strong foundation in law, policy and technology, the CIP Program seeks to enhance the security of cyber-networks, physical systems, and economic processes supporting the nation's critical infrastructures through an interdisciplinary research agenda. With the National Institute of Standards and Technology, of the Department of Commerce, serving as its executive agency, the CIP Program funds basic and applied research, as well as supports information and outreach activities related to key components of the national research agenda. During the past three years, the CIP Program has sponsored interdisciplinary and multi-institutional research within virtually every academic unit at GMU and nearly two dozen universities nationwide, including prime partner James Madison University in Harrisonburg, Virginia. In addition to many policy papers, over 270 scholarly publications have been placed in peer reviewed journals and presented in national and international forums.

In addition to basic and applied research activities, the CIP Program maintains an extensive outreach effort to highlight and advance current topical issues relevant to the national agenda. Our acclaimed *Critical Conversation Series*, held at the National Press Club in Washington, DC, and moderated by CNN Whitehouse Correspondent Frank Sesno, convenes leaders from the executive branch, Congress, industry and international organizations to discuss issues relevant to CIP. In addition to these high profile events, the CIP Program also hosts numerous workshops, seminars and conferences, focused on technology, law, economic and policy areas, and quietly convened sessions of government and private sector leaders at the behest of an outside stakeholder. Building upon this outreach and engagement strategy, the CIP Program also publishes *The CIP Report*, a monthly, electronic newsletter for professionals in industry, government, and academia who have an interest in critical infrastructure protection. Beginning as a small publication catering to those familiar with the field, the newsletter has grown to an international distribution and provides informed and timely discussion regarding the latest information about emerging legislation, government initiatives and leaders, and academic endeavors and is available online.

*The CIP Program is under the leadership of Director and Principal Investigator John A. McCarthy.*

# Center for History and New Media

Since 1994, the Center for History and New Media at George Mason University has used digital media and computer technology to democratize history—to incorporate multiple voices, reach diverse audiences, and encourage popular participation in presenting and preserving the past. CHNM combines cutting edge digital media with the latest and best historical scholarship to promote an inclusive and democratic understanding of the past as well as a broad historical literacy. CHNM's work has been recognized with major awards and grants from the American Historical Association, the National Humanities Center, the National Endowment for the Humanities, the Department of Education, the Library of Congress, and the Sloan, Hewlett, Rockefeller, Gould, Delmas, and Kellogg foundations.

## PROJECTS

CHNM maintains a wide range of online history projects directed at diverse topics and audiences. Among these are World History Matters, which helps teachers and their students locate, analyze, and learn from online primary sources; Echo: Exploring and Collecting History Online, which collects, organizes, and preserves digital materials in the history of science, technology, and industry; Interpreting the Declaration of Independence, which uses foreign translations to promote a richer understanding of the Declaration; History News Network, a web-based magazine that places current events in historical perspective; and three Teaching American History projects in collaboration with Virginia public school districts. Many of CHNM's projects have been undertaken in collaboration with the American Social History Project/Center for Media and Learning at the Graduate Center of The City University of New York. Among these collaborations are the September 11 Digital Archive, a digital repository of histories and documents of the September 11, 2001 attacks in New York, Virginia, and Pennsylvania; Liberty, Equality, Fraternity, an introduction to the French Revolution through documents and images; History Matters, a resource center and portal for U.S. history; the Lost Museum, a 3D presentation of Barnum's American Museum in 1865 in historical context; and Who Built America?, an award-winning two-volume CD-ROM.

CHNM has developed a number of online databases and other resources for historians and history teachers, including a listing of 1,200 history departments worldwide; a practical guide to Doing Digital History (forthcoming online and as a book from the University of Pennsylvania Press); a collection of essays on history and new media; and a popular set of free digital tools for historians and teachers, including Web Scrapbook, Survey Builder, Scribe, Poll Builder, and Syllabus Finder.

CHNM has made substantial contributions to teaching at George Mason University through its work with the Technology Across the Curriculum program, and the Department of History and Art History. This work has included development of online teaching modules for U.S. survey course and the Western Civilization Webography Project.

*CHNM is under the leadership of Director Roy Rosenzweig.*

# Milestones Historical Consultants

Milestones Historical Consultants was founded in the nation's capital in 1987 by historian and author Kathi Ann Brown. Services offered by Milestones range from oral history programs, historical research, and exhibit creation, to digital archive development, books, brochures, anniversary programs, and video content.

The firm's public and private sector clients from coast to coast include Fortune 100 companies, major trade associations, academic institutions, private individuals, and national museums. Among the best-known are Marriott International, Motorola, Comcast, Shell Oil, the Smithsonian, George Mason University, and the Library of Congress.

Milestones is headquartered in historic Charlottesville, Virginia, the Blue Ridge foothill town best known as the home of Thomas Jefferson's "little mountain" retreat Monticello, and the University of Virginia, an "academical village" founded and designed in 1819 by Jefferson after his retirement from public service.

Milestones founder Kathi Ann Brown is an alumna of the History Department of George Mason University, where she earned her M.A. in 1988.

*Website: www.milestonespast.com*

# John A. McCarthy

John A. McCarthy has a unique blend of executive level government, business, and academic experience in the areas of national security relative to the maritime and transportation sectors as well as in-depth knowledge of the governmental interagency process. An experienced program and crisis manager, he has been particularly successful in delivering policy and technical solutions that are time sensitive and national/international in scope.

Mr. McCarthy is Director and Principal Investigator of the Critical Infrastructure Protection (CIP) Program at the George Mason University School of Law. The CIP Project began as a $6.5M directed appropriation from the Commerce Committee to develop and implement a broad inter- and intra-university research program that supports public and private sector research needs relative to critical infrastructure and homeland security. To date, more than 70 researchers at 15 different universities have been sponsored by the CIP Program, including work in direct support of the national security agenda. Under Mr. McCarthy's leadership, the CIP Program funding has grown to over $24M in follow-on grants and has been cited by both the Governor of Virginia and federal homeland security leaders as a model academic program supporting the national CIP agenda.

Prior to joining the CIP Program, Mr. McCarthy was a Director in KPMG LLP's Mid-Atlantic Risk and Advisory Services practice in Washington, D.C., where he provided computer security, critical infrastructure, and business continuity management solutions to government clients. Prior to joining KPMG, Mr. McCarthy served as a member of the professional staff of the Critical Infrastructure Assurance Office (CIAO), which supported the National Coordinator for Security, Infrastructure Protection, and Counter-terrorism located within the National Security Council.

With more than 20 years as a commissioned officer in the United States Coast Guard, Mr. McCarthy served in a wide variety of demanding field command and senior staff positions including command-at-sea and personal Aide to 19th Commandant. During the Gulf War, Mr. McCarthy helped design and supervise United Nation sanction-enforcement operations against Iraq. He has also held numerous positions at all levels of the federal response process including pre-designated Federal

On-scene Coordinator (alternate) and Federal On-scene Coordinator's Representative under the National Contingency Plan.

Mr. McCarthy holds a B.A. degree in Psychology from The Citadel—Military College of South Carolina, Charleston, S.C., and an M.S. in Information Resource Management (specialization in government) from Syracuse University, Syracuse, N.Y. He is also a graduate of the National Defense University—Information Resource Management College, Washington, D.C., and the U.S. Naval War College— Command and Staff College, Newport, R.I. Mr. McCarthy is also a Senior Lecturer of the graduate faculty for Syracuse University's School of Information Studies, where he teaches a course on information security and critical infrastructure policy.

# Kathi Ann Brown

Kathi Ann Brown is founder of Milestones Historical Consultants, Charlottesville, Virginia. A 1980 graduate of Bryn Mawr College, Brown also holds an M.A. in History from George Mason University (GMU).

A specialist in corporate history, Brown is the author of several business, organizational and industry histories, including *The Spirit to Serve: Marriott's Way* (co-authored with J. W. Marriott, Jr.), *Make No Little Plans: The First 50 Years of the Federal City Council*, and *Wired to Win: Entrepreneurs of the American Cable Industry*. Other book clients include Motorola, Farmers Insurance, Fauquier County (VA), the Cellular Telecommunications Industry Association (CTIA), Meredith Corporation, Dewberry, CommScope and HNTB.

Brown's historical consulting practice includes oral history programs, museum exhibits, historical research, as well as digital archive and website content development. Clients include the Library of Congress, Mount Vernon, Van Kampen, Shell Oil, George Mason University, Smithsonian and GNB.

In addition to her work on *Critical Path: A Brief History of Critical Infrastructure Protection in the United States*, Brown assisted with the creation of the Critical Infrastructure Protection Digital Archive, an online historical archive developed by GMU's Center for History and New Media (CHNM) on behalf of the Critical Infrastructure Protection Program (CIPP).

In 1997, Brown was the recipient of the first Outstanding Alumnus Award given by George Mason University's Department of History.